ARCHITECTURAL
FOLLIES
IN AMERICA

1. Hexagon House, Mineral Wells, Texas.

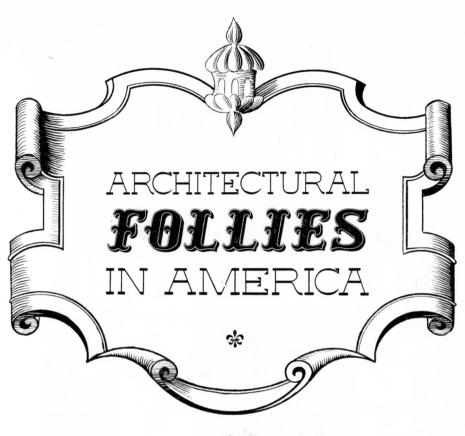

ARCHITECTURAL FOLLIES IN AMERICA

OR

HAMMER, SAW-TOOTH & NAIL

BY

CLAY LANCASTER

CHARLES E. TUTTLE COMPANY
RUTLAND, VERMONT

Published by the
Charles E. Tuttle Company of
Rutland, Vermont & Tokyo, Japan
with editorial offices at
15 Edogawa-cho, Bunkyo-ku, Tokyo

Library of Congress Catalog
Card No. 59–14088
First printing, 1960

Book design and typography by K. Ogimi
Layout of illustrations by M. Kuwata
Color plates by the Kyodo Printing Co., Tokyo
Letterpress by the Dai Nippon Printing Co., Tokyo
MANUFACTURED IN JAPAN

Gratefully dedicated to

FRANK HRUBANT

Sponsor of The House That Jack Built,
prolegomenon of the present work

CONTENTS

LIST OF ILLUSTRATIONS

Asterisks indicate color plates. All illustrations, unless otherwise indicated in their accompanying captions, are by the author.

PROLOGUE: FOLLY CONFESSIONS

EARLY in December, several years ago, I presented for the first time the material on unusual aspects of American architecture which I had been in process of collecting for a long while. The occasion was a talk given in a hall on Fifty-seventh Street in New York City, illustrated with Kodachrome slides, and billed as "The House That Jack Built." The title was quite deliberate. It was suggested by the name of a book by Eugene Clarence Gardner, *The House That Jill Built after Jack's Had Proved a Failure,* published in 1882. The main idea of the Gardner volume was that women's work qualifies them the better of the two sexes to plan where everything in the house should go. Perhaps this is true regarding some phases of planning. Yet in the original ditty about Jack and Jill it is expressly stated that Jill followed Jack in his precipitous tumble; and, with all due apologies to Mr. Gardner's pro-feminist sentiments, I am inclined to believe that the same thing applies to architecture that applies to incline descents. If men have had some pretty wild ideas about building, women have also, as will be demonstrated through examples discussed in the following pages.

I have always had a special fondness for the expression "architectural follies," and for everything indicated by the term. Having spent many happy days digging up data, poring over illustrations, reading about this fascinating subject, and searching for examples in the field, I must confess that I have also spent a comparable amount of time dreaming up my own versions to add to the accumulated store. Of course the latter have not gotten any further than on paper, but, then, neither have a lot of other of the world's most pleasant objects of contemplation. Perhaps some day I shall show them; but, for the time being, the items contained in the following collection are confined to actualized specimens.

The word "folly" has undergone a number of changes in interpretation throughout the ages, especially as applied to constructions. It seems to have come from the

French, *folie,* which originally meant "delight" or "favorite abode." There are said to be houses still existing in France that bear the antiquated epithet *La Folie.* In England, during the early part of the thirteenth century, Hubert de Burgh undertook the building of a castle near the Welsh border, and upon the completion of the foundations he ceremoniously announced that henceforth the great house would be known as "Hubert's Folly," undoubtedly Anglicizing the French equivalent. The work resumed; yet before it had gone very far the building was ordered razed to the ground by the British authorities on account of a treaty just concluded with the Welsh. As the demolition proceeded much amusement was manifested among the country folk, who remarked that the builder had proved himself a true prophet in the selection of title for his establishment.* "Folly" now had an English denotation.

The two meanings of the word "folly" persevered side by side. In the original connotation it became more and more closely linked with gardens and garden summerhouses or kiosks, especially with the abundance of them erected in England during the eighteenth century.† Up to about the beginning of the 1900's it continued to be applied to public pleasure gardens in some parts, and then faded into disuse. In France it was last employed with any regularity for designating small country houses where people disported themselves freely; but for this, too, it has become obsolete. However, the alternative meaning has increased in popularity since medieval times. In the *Monthly Magazine* for 20 February 1796 a British gentleman complained that he had "built a great many mounds in the form of sugar-loaves, very broad at bottom and pointed at top," and that travelers began calling them his "folly." The appellation is presumed to have been uncomplimentary, indicating the man's foolishness in what he did. Strictly speaking, "folly" has come to refer to any costly structure considered to have shown folly in the builder.

Nowhere have buildings been labeled follies more liberally than in America. Here a folly was a building offensive to the sense of good taste and restraint, or simply one out of key with its neighbors in size, style, or planning. The word was especially brought to bear upon cases where the builder either underestimated the cost of construction or overestimated his own resources counted upon to finance the project, which remained unfinished as a consequence. Sometimes "folly" was applied to a building in which a series of unforeseen events played havoc with the intended course of operations and there ensued a minor bedlam reminiscent of the occurrences befalling

* *A New Dictionary on Historical Principles,* Oxford, 1901, Vol. IV, p. 393.
† Barbara Jones, *Follies and Grottoes,* London, 1953.

the animal occupants of a dwelling erected by a certain builder named Jack, the whole account written up in that all-time favorite nursery book entitled *Mother Goose*. Considering these viewpoints all together, and picking out the various structures that would be qualified by them, we have in each and every one of them the house that Jack built.

Shortly after the talk mentioned at the beginning, a group of my architectural curiosities was published in the magazine *American Heritage* under the heading "Architectural Follies," the illustrations printed in halftone, with brief accompanying descriptions.* Upon seeing it in print I was struck by the desire to expand the material into a book, which has resulted in the present enterprise. As every author knows, the most important words he writes are those that go onto the cover and spine of the book to enable the bibliophile to extract the right volume from the shelf. It was unthinkable of calling the book *The House That Jack Built,* because bookshops and libraries immediately would banish it to the juvenile department, there to cool its heels indefinitely. Although this undoubtedly would preserve each copy for future generations it was not in line with the object of having it published. Bestowing upon the book the lone title of *Architectural Follies* seemed a bit confusing, inasmuch as the second word suggests to the casual observer a particular species of stage entertainment made famous several decades back by Flo Ziegfeld, and therefore unrelated to the subject dealt with in the current opus. As has been said, I like the term "architectural follies," but using it for a title seemed to require some supplementation. What was really needed was a good sub-title. My problem was getting the right one.

Whenever I am faced by such a dilemma I find a workable method of solution is to stand up, walk about a bit, and make gestures with the hands sympathetic to the mood that is to be conveyed. It seems that acting something out facilitates finding the right words. In this episode I first pointed in the direction of imaginary bulging domes atop a bizarre villa at Bridgeport, Connecticut, built by one obscure(?) gentleman calling himself P. T. Barnum, gave a gentle wave to indicate the fancy lacework on a wedding-cake house at Kennebunk, Maine, made several repetitious thrusts supposed to signify the continuous building operations of the Winchester abode of mystery—the rifle residence at San Jose, California—and then brought the demonstration to a conclusion with various polygons drawn in the ether in memory of the phrenologist pace-setter of mid-nineteenth-century house design, Orson Squire Fowler, who conceived a residence many persons considered rather odious at Fishkill, New York. "The

* Vol. I, no. 2, Winter 1953–54, pp. 6–/11/.

thing that characterizes all these works," I announced to myself, "is the seriousness and intensity by which the builders tackled their tasks. They went at it tooth and claw!" Then I brought the back of my right hand down into the palm of the left, resulting in a smack that sounded like the blow of a hammer. Now from this point on the reader can easily reconstruct my reasoning. With an attitude of tooth and claw in mind and the reverberation of a hammer-sound ringing in my ears, it was only a matter of a few percolations of thought waves before the required sub-title was all ready to be set down on a little card and filed away until time for it to be brought out and emblazoned on the finished manuscript. The letters inscribed on the little card said:

HAMMER, SAW,
TOOTH & NAIL.

THE FOLLY
TRADITION

IT IS to be noted that many of the architectural follies produced in America bear a relationship to follies that have been launched in the Old World. In a few instances—such as Mrs. Trollope's bazaar, Barnum's "Iranistan," and the Leaning Tower of Niles—the American versions are known to have had a direct connection with specific examples abroad; but usually their being of like form is a matter of following certain patterns engaged in on former occasions, coincidentally taken up again. For man is man the world around, and his likes and dislikes, his glories and foibles are returned to by other individuals time after time, the results differing mainly because circumstances and conditions differ between one place and another as the centuries roll by, though the intent remains the same.

By way of introduction to the American follies this first chapter offers a brief discussion of a selection of six foreign follies, that have come to be considered classics after their fashion. They represent a wide distribution, from about the third millennium B.C. to the nineteenth century of our era, including one from the Far East, one from the Near East, one from the Mediterranean, and one each from France, Bavaria, and England. The reader will find repeated references in later chapters to the half-dozen key examples here presented, which justifies and explains why these particular ones have been picked out for special analysis. Also, mention will be made of others, as occasions arise, in the main body of the text. These will be found listed, along with all the American follies either described in some degree of fullness or only casually cited, in the index at the back of the book. Additional follies are included in the appendix, a geographical listing of all American follies known to the author. Of course no attempt is made to cover the field of follies outside of the United States; indeed, such an undertaking would turn out to be of cyclopedic proportions, involving a far greater amount of material than could possibly be squeezed into the present volume,

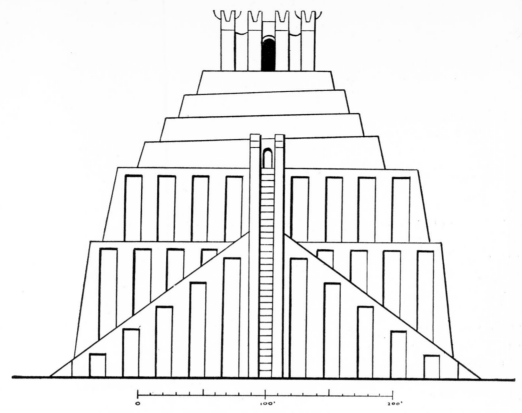

2. Elevation of the "Tower of Babel," reconstructed from a cuneiform inscription of about 229 B.C. After Eckhard Unger, Assyrische und Babylonische Kunst, Breslau, 1927, Plate 104.

which sets out to concentrate on the New World collection. The inclusion of the six foreign examples that follow does not aspire to accomplish anything more penetrating than to give some inkling of the nature of the many constructions they represent, these being the predecessors to the architectural follies erected in the United States.*

THE TOWER OF BABEL

THE MOST famous of all follies of antiquity is the legendary Tower of Babel, which, according to the eleventh chapter of Genesis, was begun on the Plain of Shinar, wherever that may have been. The tower—or city—came into being as a means of explaining the prevalence of so many languages after the world had been repopulated by a single family saved from the devastating waters of the flood in the ark that Noah, in one of his sober periods, had had the industry to construct. In this regard the name "Babel" is associated with the Hebrew word *bālal,* meaning "to confuse," referring, of course, to the confusion of tongues.

The people, it seems, were desirous of erecting a great structure whose summit

* It might be well to mention at this point that the reader will find reference works cited in the notes from time to time. Attention is called to the omission of the state and city guides compiled by the Federal Writers' Project of the W. P. A., published during the 1930's and 1940's. Most of the follies in existence at that time are included in these books, which, however, constitute such an obvious place to look for material on unusual buildings that it seems superfluous to refer to them in each specific instance. The entire collection is recommended here for the factual material presented.

would reach up to heaven. The materials they employed were certainly primitive: dried mud bricks and slime. But they must have been getting along fairly well in the project and had attained some measure of success when their endeavor was halted by a disaster inflicted upon them by the very deity they were striving to reach. The result was that they began speaking different languages and became scattered throughout the earth. What a magnificent folly they must have left behind them!

The biblical incident was brought up in the proceedings of a British court of law a little over a hundred years ago, which tends to throw some light upon what may have been the disorganizing factor in the enterprise.

It seems that Mr. Alexander, the architect of Rochester Bridge and other buildings in the County of Kent, was under cross-examination in a special jury case at Maidstone. His interlocutor was bent upon detracting from the weight of his testimony; and after the usual preliminaries the give-and-take ran something like this:

"You are a builder, I believe?"

"No sir; I am not a builder—I am an architect!"

"Ah well? architect or builder, builder or architect, they are much the same I suppose?"

"I beg your pardon sir—I cannot admit that; I consider them to be totally different!"

"Oh, indeed! Perhaps you will state wherein this great difference consists?"

"An architect, sir, prepares the plans, conceives the design, draws out the specifications—in short, supplies the mind. The builder is merely the bricklayer or the carpenter; the builder in fact is the machine—the architect the power that puts the machine together, and sets it going..."

"Oh, very well, Mr. Architect—that will do! and now, after your very ingenious distinction without a difference, perhaps you could inform the court who was the architect of the Tower of Babel?"

And now mark the reply—which, for promptness and wit, is perhaps not to be rivalled in the whole history of rejoinder.

"There was no architect, sir—and hence the confusion!"*

Disregarding the cause given for the failure of the building project our curiosity is still unsatisfied as to where the tower was and what it was like. It has been suggested that Shinar is Sumer, in the lower valley of the Euphrates River. Some of the earliest manifestations of sophisticated civilization are attributed to the Sumerians, various art forms and the invention of cuneiform writing, adopted by all the later nations in this area. Dominating all their constructions was the great square ziggurat, or stepped

* *Kentucky Statesman*, 16 June 1857, p. 1.

temple-tower, such as that at Ur, originally built late in the third millennium B.C. Constructed of earth and crude brick (in which respect it accords with the description of the Tower of Babel) the structure was surfaced, however, with layers of baked brick laid in bitumen (mineral pitch—a better adhesive substance than slime). The walls sloped inward somewhat and all lines were given a slight convexity to relieve the optical illusion of sag one gets in extended straight planes and contours. On one side three staircases of one-hundred steps each rose to a common pinnacle, at which point was located a gateway opening in front of the shrine set on a square terrace. The overall height of the structure was upwards of ninety feet. Color was applied to the ziggurat: perhaps black at the base denoting the underworld, red for the middle stage representing the earth, blue for the sky above, and finally gold for the heavenly body principally honored, which in this case was Nannar, the moon god and ruler of the kingdom. The ziggurat at Ur is in a ruined state today, known locally as al Muqayyar, "Mount of Pitch," from the prevalence of the binding substance found round about it.

A similar structure, that actually has been called "Tower of Babel," is located upon the site of old Babylon, the sound of which name very well may have been echoed in the word "Babel." This also is a ziggurat, and it was standing in the days of Hammurabi, the great law-giver of the eighteenth or seventeenth century B.C. The ziggurat was known then at Etemenanki, "The House of the Terrace-platform of Heaven and Earth." It was dedicated to Marduk (Merodach in the Bible), the tutelary divinity of the city of Babylon. In a more ruinous state than its predecessor at Ur, the monument at Babylon—or Tower of Babel—according to an ancient (though relatively late) inscription, displayed most of the features of the earlier ziggurat; yet it was larger in every respect, covering an area over half again as great and rising three times its height. Repeating the three stairways, the subsidiary pair led to a platform lower than that of the axial staircase, which ascended precipitously to the base of a ramp-pyramid around which one wound four times up to the topmost terrace where stood the shrine of Marduk.

The ziggurat is located to the north of what was the city of Babylon, once connected by a procession street leading to the famous Ishtar Gate, and nearby were the more famous Hanging Gardens built by Nebuchadnezzar. The structures cited must have impressed the Jews in the city of their captivity. Here were soaring, artificial mountains—the hill-dwelling of the god and hill-gardens for the pleasure of the court—created in sharp contrast to the featureless plain, all of them having a flavor of folly about them.

Whether from Sumer or Babylon, the inspiration for the Tower of Babel (like the flood that preceded it) seems to have come from across the river in Mesopotamia. To a people of nomadic tendencies, with little aptitude for building, though much literary inventiveness, the spectacle of the towering ziggurat furnished considerable material for speculation, and so became featured in a story purporting to explain the origin of all languages.

THE VILLA PALAGONIA

WHETHER or not the Tower of Babel proved once and for all the futility of building follies as group projects is difficult to say. Suffice it is to note that subsequent examples were individually conceived and sponsored, though of course requiring the efforts of a great many persons to carry them out. The uniqueness of the buildings is usually matched—and sometimes exceeded—by the odd doings of their patrons, which brings us to the subject of the Villa Palagonia and the gouty prince who was responsible for the weird character it assumed. The eighteenth-century prince has passed into the world of legend, remembered in conflicting accounts; but his former home survives, though at present it has come down in the world from a princely habitation to a series of cold-water flats sparsely tenanted by bachelor bourgeois.

There was a time when the Villa Palagonia at Bagheria, Sicily, was a respectable and even pretentious building, far more attractive than its master, Ferdinando Francesca Gravina, Prince of Palagonia, who had a long string of impressive titles after his name and ample wealth at his bidding, but nothing else to recommend him. At the time he set about to remodel his paternal residence he was well advanced in years, pockmarked and misshapen, and maintained an unsavory reputation among his neighbors for maltreatment of his servants. Somehow—perhaps due to persisting human optimism or the allure of the man's physical possessions outweighing his physical appearance—the Prince of Palagonia managed to win the hand of the beautiful sixteen-year-old Maria Gioachina Gaetani, whose popularity brought scores of gay acquaintances and not a few admirers into the palazzo. If it were the exuberance of Maria that instituted rounds of entertainments for her friends, it was the jealousy of her mismatched husband that put an end to them. Whether justified or not he suspected her of illicit conduct and set about to try to keep her under lock and key. But she was young and vivacious, and somehow always managed to escape into the Sicilian moonlit

3. Entrance gateway to the Villa Palagonia, Bagheria, Sicily.

nights to keep her rendezvous. The prince brooded over means of retaining her indoors, and showed signs of becoming obsessed.

The plan he hit upon was curious in just the right degree one would expect from a warped mind. From Palermo were hired a number of stone carvers, and under the supervision of a Dominican friar named Tommaso di Napoli and one Agatino Daidone, they cut out of the local porus brown coral weird monsters with faces set in frozen grimaces; and in the middle of the night the stone grotesques were rolled into the bedroom of Maria, who was awakened with a start, confronted by the improvised nightmares! Afterwards, the figures were stationed beside the gates, atop the walls, and along the alleys in the garden, where they would frighten anyone coming upon them unsuspectedly. More in the sense of bragging over his thwarted triumph than out of charity it is said that on the road approaching the villa the prince had a sign posted warning expectant mothers to beware less the sight of the carved demons ahead should cause them to give birth to abnormal babies.

The villa was visited and described by several eighteenth-century notables, among them the French metallurgist and historian Michel Jean Comte de Borch and the German writer Johann Wolfgang von Goethe, the latter seeing the Villa Palagonia on his tour of Sicily in 1787, the year before the prince died. In his *Travels* Goethe described "Prince Pallagonia's folly" as the "most tasteless...of erections":

"The passage to the castle is broader than usual, the wall being converted into a continuous socle; from which basement the strangest groups possible reach to the top. ... The ugliest of these unshapely figures (the bungling work of the most ordinary mason,) is increased by their having been cut out of a very crumbly muscheltufa. ...

"We now approach the castle and are received into a semi-circular fore-court. The chief wall before us, through which is the entrance door, is in the castle style. Here we find an Egyptian figure built into the wall, a fountain without water, a monument, vases stuck around in no sort of order. ... Next we come to the castle court, and found the usual round area, enclosed with little cottages, distorted into small semicircles. ...

"The absurdities produced by such want of judgment and taste, however, are strikingly instanced by the fact, that the window sills in these cottages are, without exception, oblique, and lean to one side or the other, so as to offend and violate all sense of the level and perpendicular. ... And then, again, the edges of all the roofs are *embellished* with hydras and little busts, with choirs of monkeys playing music, and similar conceits. Dragons alternate with deities. ..."

Goethe was permitted inside the villa, "which, having been built by the father, presents relatively a more rational appearance than the exterior." However, he finds that alterations have been made in a peculiar sort of provincial richness. His attention centers on the furniture, where "the madness of the prince begins again to rave. Many of the seats have lost their legs, so that no one can sit upon them; and if some appear to promise a resting-place, the Chamberlain warns you against them, as having sharp prickles beneath their satin-covered cushions."*

The main apartment in the villa is the ballroom, now empty except for its bizarre décor. The walls of varicolored marbles are frosted over with scroll moldings and shell forms, and affixed to odd-shaped panels are busts of the prince's ancestors, in full round, staring out in space or gesticulating arrogantly at one another. The deep cove of

* *Goethe's Travels in Italy* (translated by A. J. W. Morrison and Charles Nisbet), London, 1892, pp. 232–34.

4. Corner of the ballroom in the Villa Palagonia.

the ceiling is lavishly embellished with paintings in which waterbirds, horses, and other creatures come bounding through the architectural motifs out of nowhere, enlivening the upper regions of the room; and the ceiling proper is plated with mirrors that reflect and reduplicate the carved and painted fantasies below in confusing inversion—if indeed such materialized flights of the imagination could be more deranging upside down than rightside up. The ballroom climaxes the design-intent of the whole villa—a display of diabolic distortions, whereby the mad Prince of Palagonia expressed resentment over his sad condition in terms at once tense, tempestuous, tawdry, and tasteless.

DÉSERT DE RETZ

NOT FAR from Paris, on the outskirts of the Forest of Marly, stands the ruins of a strange construction that teases the imagination. It is in the form of a truncated column, but a column of extraordinary proportions—forty-five feet in diameter. The base is sunken into the ground, and one looks in vain for the remains of other columns to what must have been a gigantic classic temple three times the height of the façade of the Cathedral of Notre Dame; but it is all in vain, for nothing of the kind ever existed more than the stump of the one pillar that has been mentioned. It was, indeed, an entire building in itself, a dwelling of four stories above ground level and two below, averaging six rooms to a floor, not counting the numerous closets and service rooms.

The building was the *folie* of François Racine de Monville, a French grandee holding a subordinate though lucrative position at the court of Louis XVI and bearing the title *Huissier de la Chambre du Roi*. M. de Monville was an artist on a dilettante level: he played the harp, showed some skill at archery, and did very well as a draftsman. In the last capacity he may have taken a hand in planning his own house, aided by the gifted Hubert Robert, a landscape painter of considerable note and officially the *Dessinateur des Jardins du Roi*. The de Monville project embraced more than a single house in the shape of a broken column, being a private park of manifold delights.

The estate at Marly was a large irregular plot enclosed by a wall, laid out in 1771; and in 1785 a number of engravings of plans, sections, elevations, and perspective views were issued in the thirteenth volume of Le Rouge's famous *Jardins Anglo-Chinois*, which was a fitting publication inasmuch as the main idea for the scheme had come from the new informal gardening system currently popular in England, inspired in turn by the Chinese. Although quite different from the symmetrical planning of continental gardens, there was a strongly French touch to everything created here by de Monville and Robert. The place originally was called Le Désert (Wilderness) de Monville, and somehow later came to be referred to as the Désert de Raye or Désert de Retz, alias the "Jardin Anglais."

6   12   18   24   30 Pieds.

Coupe du Levant au Couchant avec construction pour les Caves.

5. Cross-section of the column residence of M. de Monville.
From George Louis le Rouge, *Détails des Nouveaux Jardins à la Mode et Jardins Anglo-chinois.* Vol. XIII, Paris, 1785.

The principal entrance to the park was in the northeast wall at the point nearest the column. The gateway was a rustic affair, like a grotto or like a Chinese garden of grotesquely shaped stones. One of the Le Rouge engravings shows some visitors entering at night, their way illuminated by torches held by two fauns stationed at either side of the entrance; but one cannot tell whether the torchbearers are bronze figures or servants masquerading for the occasion. A hundred feet to the northwest of the column was an open-air theatre, and beyond, on the other side of the winding path, was a Tuscan-style temple to the god Pan, with a half-circular portico in front of a rectangular cella. The path divided a little farther on, each branch leading to secondary entrances to the Désert.

Below the column were the commune, or out-buildings, the greenhouses, and some-

la Colonne.

6. M. de Monville's column.
From le Rouge.

what to the west an orangery. A thatched cottage stood close by, and between the cottage and greenhouses was an exotic Chinese house, the second most important structure in the park. It was, however, not like any existing Chinese building, but seemed to have been taken from some *chinoiserie* ornamental design on porcelain. The exterior appeared three stories tall (the top in reality a clerestory to the second floor), crowned by curvilinear roofs with bells at the jutting corners, vases for chimneys (unheard of in China of course), imitation bamboo posts and brackets, lattice grilles everywhere; and the interior was completely French! The Chinese house had its own wriggly little garden that tumbled down to a small lake. A somewhat larger lake farther to the south contained an island called the Isle of Happiness (Isle du Bonheur). Following the labyrinth of interpenetrating paths to the south and east one came upon

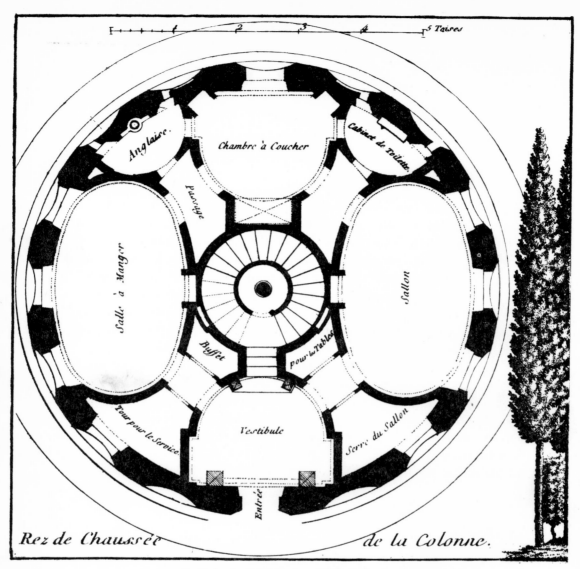

7. Principal floor plan of the column.
From le Rouge.

a mastaba-like tomb embellished with nude figures, a hermitage, and—in the eastern section—an obelisk. Wandering back toward the main house one passed the dairy and farm group, and (as though one had not been exposed to enough architectural variety already) the mock ruin of a gothic church and an icehouse in the form of a pyramid, the last more Roman than Egyptian.

The fragmentary column itself was one of the most daring follies of the eighteenth century in Europe. The windows—vertical rectangles on the main floor, square on the second, oval on the third—were arranged in the sixteen flutings of the shaft. Clerestory fenestration provided light for the rooms on the top story. The central circular staircase around an open well was skylighted. On the principal floor were the elliptical salon and dining room, semicircular chamber with its adjoining necessities, a curved-end entrance vestibule and several odd-shaped service rooms. On the floors above the rooms were arranged in suites composed of curved salons and bedrooms with recessed bed alcoves. The fourth floor contained a studio, off which opened shops for wood and metal working, servants' rooms, and a storage garret. Offices, kitchens, and cellars occupied the underground levels. Although many of the room shapes were peculiar there was little waste space due to the central location of the staircase serving as an axis for communication to all parts of the building. None of the rooms was very large, the main living and dining rooms measuring only about fourteen by twenty-one feet, the ceiling height here eleven feet, and eight for the upper stories.

During the intervening years the jagged skyline of the column has been evened up and windows cut through the outer wall to provide more light and air for the top apartments. Yet, counteracting the attempts man has made to deprive the column of its rustic character, nature has stepped in to further irregularize the now-abandoned construction, sending vines and creepers swarming over its walls, staining and marring every surface, and poking out the panes of glass so that today the hollow windows stare out blankly at the unchecked verdancy that besieges M. de Monville's *folie*.

THE PALACE AT BRIGHTON

AS SUGGESTED by the Chinese house near the column of M. de Monville, when the French wished to be exotic they turned for inspiration to China, whence came the exquisite silks and porcelains of which they were so fond; the English, on the other hand, turned to India, taking pride in their enormous territorial possessions in south Asia, that had kept their pockets so well lined since initial negotiations made during the reign of Queen Elizabeth. The adaptation of the Indian style came about in large measure due to a number of books filled with colored plates showing views in India, the most influential of which were drawn and engraved by Thomas Daniell and published during the closing years of the eighteenth and first decade of the nineteenth century, including: *Antiquities of India* (1790), *Oriental Scenery* (1795), *Hindoo Excavations in the Mountain of Ellora* (1803), and *A Picturesque Voyage to India; by the Way of China* (1810). Not only were painted murals, wallpaper, and other decorative uses derived from the Daniell plates, but, as we shall see, a good-sized residence and an imperial palace as well.

Thomas Daniell himself had a share in bringing into being the country villa built

Drawn & Etched by C.Moore.

PAVILION,

FRONT TOWARDS THE STEINE,

JOHN NASH, ESQ? ARCHIT & INVENT

London, Published April 1824, by John Nash, Esq? & Sold by R.Ackerman

about 1805 for Sir Charles Cockerell, who had lived in India with his brother, Samuel
Pepys Cockerell, architect and surveyor to the East India House and the actual de-
lineator of the architectural plans. Daniell's work probably had to do mostly with the
gardens. The Indian-style house, called Sezincote, was constructed in Gloucestershire.
It was classical in plan yet Mughal in all of its external details of lobated windows,

T. Sutherland. Acqua.

8. *The remodeled Palace at Brighton.*
From Edward Wedlake Bradley, *Illustrations of Her Majesty's Palace at Brighton,* London, 1838.

minaret-like pinnacles and turquoise-colored copper dome.* Another gentleman who took part in the creation of Sezincote was Humphrey Repton.

Just as Louis XIV had been so enchanted by the Château of Vaux-le-Vicomte that he

* Christopher Hussey, "Sezincote," *Country Life,* 13 May 1939, pp. 502–6; *ibid.,* 20 May 1939, pp. 528–32.

summoned the designers to Versailles to enlarge his father's old hunting lodge into a sprawling palace, so the English Prince (later George IV) commanded Humphrey Repton to come to Brighton to discuss plans for remodeling the Marine Pavilion into a suitable royal residence of an unusual design. Begun in 1784 after a design by Henry Holland, and added to in 1801–2, the Marine Pavilion was composed of a round-domed central mass surrounded by an Ionic colonnade, with rectangular wings of two stories to either side, the latter having the appearance of squeezing the unit between them. Also there was a huge domed stable, just completed by William Porden before Repton's visit in 1805, that Repton thought looked like a Turkish mosque. The buildings had possibilities though the land was rather restricted. Due to the building boom that had taken place since Brighton had been favored with royal patronage, private houses were crowding about the prince's property on all sides. After inspecting the existing structures Repton set about to render his proposal for changes and additions, the result turning out to be an architectural extravaganza based on Indian forms, featuring bulbous domes, balconies, open pavilions, pointed windows, and long glazed galleries that were made to look unlimited in length through the placing of a full-length mirror at the intersection in such a way as to reflect the gallery extension set at right angles as though it were continuous in a straight line. The prince was delighted with the design and declared: "Mr. Repton...I consider the whole of this work as perfect, and will have every part of it carried into immediate execution; not a tittle shall be altered— even you yourself shall not attempt an improvement."* But the predictions of even the high and mighty may not come true! A gust of national economy cooled the prince's intentions and the project was laid aside. Repton, naturally, was disappointed; and in 1808 he published his *Designs for the Pavillon at Brighton* to show the world in brilliant polychromy what his princely would-be patron might have had if his plans had followed through. The plates had cutout flaps that could be turned back, illustrating what various views were like in their existing condition, and how they would look had Repton's genius been brought to bear upon them.

Although the prince had been made to postpone the realization of an exotic dream at Brighton it was not abandoned permanently. In less than a decade he returned to the venture, acquiring adjoining property in 1815 and instructing John Nash, who held the office of Surveyor General, to restudy the Marine Pavilion and see what could be done about making it over into a veritable Eastern potentate's palace. Nash's scheme was larger and more fanciful than Repton's had been. On the side toward the Steine the original round salon in the middle was made into an imposing element through an ex-

* John Summerson, *John Nash*, London, 1935, pp. 160–61.

change of the old plain encircling porch for a new one having open work above horse-shoe arches, the cylindrical form crowned by a tremendous bulbous dome, and the chimneystacks heightened into slim minarets. A similar treatment was given to the rectangular wings, including smaller onion domes with fancy finials atop each one. Large square blocks were constructed at both ends to house the great banqueting hall and music room, the tall windows sheltered by an arcade similar to that of the middle section, the roof rising into a concave conical form, the minaret motifs repeated at each of the four corners. The main part of the building was transformed or added to between 1818 and 1821, though work continued for several years more. It was an extravagant undertaking costing over £500,000, of which about £146,000 went for decorations and furnishings. John Nash's commission was £4,646, a sizeable figure for an architect's fee in those days.

There was no purity of design in the remodeled Brighton Palace. The pointed windows and roofs of the great, square end pavilions were more gothic than Indian, as were the use of pinnacles and the rows of chimney stacks. Inside there was a strong flavor of the Far East. The Chinese Gallery located immediately behind the round salon was 17 feet wide and 162 feet long, with trelliswork much in evidence and a chimney-piece of brass and iron simulating bamboo, with Chinese canopies in the upper parts, dragons and other motifs in stained glass, and over-life-size statues of mandarins standing in niches. Opening off one end of the Chinese Gallery was the Music Room, which was forty-two feet square with ten-foot recesses on two sides, having an octagonal coved ceiling surmounted by a dome from which were suspended a number of chandeliers that looked like glowing yellow flowers. Dragons held up the heavy blue draperies of the five windows, between which stood four porcelain pagodas; and another pair flanked the fireplace opposite. At the far end of the long gallery was located the great Banqueting Room with big Chinese figures painted on the walls. From the necks of phoenix birds or peacocks in each of the pendentives of the ceiling were hung jeweled chandeliers; and a large central one with small dragons holding tulip lamps in their mouths, clutched in the claws of a big dragon amidst a cluster of banana leaves at the apex of the dome. The dragon motif also appeared in the panels of the overdoors and elsewhere throughout the decoration, making the hall into a veritable dragon's den. The prince entertained lavishly, as befitted the setting, and there was built up an aura of traditions around the Palace at Brighton that lent additional glamour to the picturesque architectural pile, the appearance of which alone is sufficiently fascinating to maintain a renewing interest in the building by the general public generation after generation.

THE "EUROPEAN PALACES" OF YÜAN MING YÜAN

THE ROMANTIC urge to build exotic pavilions was not restricted to the West but existed also in tl Far East. In the same way that designers exploited Oriental forms in devising escapist architecture in Europe, so, in the Orient too, use was made of European styles for a comparable bizarre effect—which is fair exchange. The eighteenth-century European-type buildings in China could be found in a relatively small area, it being the exclusive prerogative of the emperor to indulge in such a frivolous and expensive recreation. His Hsi Yang Lou (literally "Western Sea Palaces") or "European Palaces" were built in three enclosures at the northeast corner of Yüan Ming Yüan ("Round Bright Garden"), the Versailles of the Flowery Kingdom, located about six miles northwest of Peking.

When Emperor Ch'ien Lung came to the throne in 1735 he inherited, among many other things from his predecessors, an Italian artist by the name of Joseph (Giuseppe) Castiglione, who was a member of the Jesuit Society. Brother Castiglione had come to China in 1715 as a missionary; but the court had given him little chance to demonstrate his powers of religious persuasion, although making much use of his artistic talents. Castiglione's partner in bringing about the "European Palaces" group was his confrere, Father Michel Benoît, who conceived the fountains, which so captivated the imagination of the emperor that the buildings almost may be said to have been erected merely as appropriate settings for the water displays. Father Benoît was a newcomer to China, arriving in 1745, or two years before the undertaking of the foreign palaces. He had made a model of a fountain, that was presented to the emperor and kept in the royal apartment where he could amuse himself with it as a plaything.

The first building erected was called Hsieh Ch'i Ch'ü, which may be translated as "Harmonious Wonderful Pleasing," a name as romantic as the edifice to which it referred. The structure was composed of a central rectangular block of three parts on an elevated basement that was extended out into hemicycles on two sides, terminating in two-storied octagonal pavilions. In the court thus formed a double staircase descended in curved flights to the brim of a basin populated by sculptured animals that spouted jets of water into the pool. There was a lake beyond a balustrade at the edge of a terrace, and here the emperor loved to sit and watch the dancing of the fountains fed by water from a reservoir housed in a building to the north. Musicians stationed in the octagonal pavilions played native Chinese music and tunes imported from Tibet,

Mongolia, and Turkestan. The "palace" was built of brick covered with stucco painted a brilliant vermilion, with white marble pilasters set with gilded brass ornaments, and the roof overlaid with glazed tiles of green, red, royal yellow, blue, and violet. Hsieh Ch'i Ch'ü bore some resemblance to French *chinoiserie* architecture, such as the Trianon de Porcelaine, the first Chinese essay of any importance in Europe, built for Louis XIV between 1670 and 1672, and taken down fifteen years later because its "porcelain" facing was not weatherproof.* The use of the hemicycles as orangeries further suggests Versailles. Although the central structure looked to be two stories high, above the basement, it was but one (which is consistent with the Chinese practice of avoiding multistoried buildings wherever possible. Also typically Chinese was the fact that the thick masonry walls were built around wooden posts holding up the roof timbers, rather than themselves carrying the weight of the superstructure. The relationship of building to fountains was just the reverse of what it was in Europe, where one looked at the fountains playing from inside and not from a point beyond as here, the building becoming a backdrop to the waterworks. The association of fountains to architecture can be seen in an engraving of the first palace taken from a set showing his Western buildings ordered by the emperor in 1786. This engraving served as the basis for our illustration. One notes how excessively ornamented the building is.

The balance of the "European Palaces" group was in the same exuberant manner. The principal entrance from the Chinese part of the garden was through a gateway featuring a clock over the opening (seen in part at the extreme left of our view). One found himself upon a bridge of five arches having keystones carved into grotesque masks emitting water through their mouths into the lake. From the bridge a fine view could be had of the south court of Hsieh Ch'i Ch'ü. Above this building extended the second enclosure devoted to a flower garden featuring a labyrinth with an elevated eight-sided kiosk in the center serving as a lookout for the emperor to watch his concubines losing themselves in the maze.

The third and largest enclosure to the east was accessible through an aviary. The main pavilion in this group was called Hai Yen T'ang, or the "Palace of the Calm Sea," the most impressive building in the foreign style. Once again we find the fountains combined with the double staircase, here spreading out in an open V-formation, with jets of water set into the balustrade; and bordering the pool below were large bronze castings of the twelve Chinese cyclical animals, each one made to spurt water from its mouth during the two-hour period of the day assigned to it, and all gushing in unison

* For a comparison between the "European Palaces" of Ch'ien Lung and European Baroque examples see the author's "The 'European Palaces' of Yüan Ming Yüan," *Gazette des Beaux-Arts,* October 1948, pp. /261/–288.

at high noon. Neighboring buildings consisted of the belvedere, the "Bamboo Court" (in Chinese style) and a gallery erected in 1767 for exhibiting some Gobelin tapestries presented to Ch'ien Lung by Louis XV. Facing the tapestry building was a throne platform with a carved screen of marble behind it, and in the middle area was a pair of giant fountains in the shape of pagodas. When the water was released the noise was so terrific that one could not hear another person's voice though he shouted in his ear. To the east were triumphal arches on the near and far sides of a mount, on top of which was perched a gazebo; and completing the attractions of the third enclosure was an open-air theatre, for which Brother Castiglione was charged with designing and painting scenery when not busy on matters pertaining to building.

9. Hsieh Ch'i Ch'ü, first of the Western-style palaces erected at Yüan Ming Yüan by Castiglione in 1747.

The dénouement of the "European Palaces" group is rather distressing. After the decease of the engineer, Father Benoît, in 1774, the mechanism that supplied the water tanks broke down, and, there being no one who knew how to fix the apparatus, the tanks had to be filled by a bucket brigade, which, however, did serve to relieve the unemployment situation in China at that time. Little use was made of the area after the passing of Ch'ien Lung in 1795. The fatal blow to the buildings fell in October of 1860, when the British, as a reprisal, burned all of Yüan Ming Yüan and carried off the furnishings as plunder, some of which is shamelessly displayed in the galleries of the British Museum. Afterwards, the charred remains of the masonry of the foreign-style palaces reverted into quarries for the local peasantry seeking building materials.

THE CASTLES OF LUDWIG II

A CENTURY after the Chinese emperor ordered engravings made of the Western-style palaces and but shortly after these same buildings were destroyed by the British, a European monarch admired them so much that he proposed building copies of them for his own diversion. It would have been a magnificent boomerang!—only, for economic reasons, it never happened. The European monarch had to content himself with wandering through such piles of romantic architecture as he already possessed.

The wanderer in question was Ludwig II, who, at the age of eighteen, had succeeded his father, Maximilian II, to the crown of Bavaria in 1864. Ludwig and the Chinese ruler had one thing in common and that was seeking entertainment in solitude, which, although traditional for Chinese emperors, was due to a melancholy disposition on the part of Ludwig. He and his brother Otto had been given a private classical education void of any provision for sports or physical activities that might have served to alleviate their introvert tendencies; and, as time went on, Ludwig turned more and more toward indulging his tastes for music, theatricals, and building dream castles. Early in his career he formed an attachment for the German composer Richard Wagner, almost thirty years his senior, who, for about twenty months, was his guest and constant companion. Through Ludwig's generosity Wagner's past debts and proposed artistic utopias came to be a drain on the Bavarian national treasury; and these, combined with his foreign origin, and what was considered an unwholesome influence of Wagner upon the king, led to a state decree forcing Ludwig to give up the one person he had befriended. However, Ludwig often stole off to the opera house in Munich or Bayreuth to hear the Wagnerian operas, sometimes being so bold as to invite Wagner to sit in his box.

Next to Wagner, Ludwig admired most the eighteenth-century French queen Marie Antoinette, and kept her marble likeness next his bed where he could see it first thing upon waking in the morning. His devotion led him to have her palace retreat, the Petit Trianon, interpreted at Linderhof, originally a hunting lodge built for Maximilian deep in the Bavarian highlands. Ludwig sent to France for models to be made of everything used by Marie Antoinette, and from these his designers spent from 1869 to 1879 fashioning the new *folie*. It contained ten reception rooms and one bedroom. The prevailing color was a forget-me-not blue. Other attractions developed at Linderhof were: an imitation of the grotto at Capri made of cement and brown linen, specially lighted at night

10. The castle Neuschwanstein at Marienbrücke, Bavaria.

by means of the first electricity plant in Bavaria; a pavilion nearby called Hunding's Hut; the Hermitage of Gurnemanz; a lake on which a pair of mechanical swans pulled a barge on which Ludwig bedecked himself as Lohengrin for moonlight excursions; a Moorish kiosk set high on a mountain where the king retired dressed in Eastern costume; and a terraced garden leading up to the great linden tree that lent its name to the estate, a staircase in its hollow trunk ascending to an observatory.

Linderhof hardly satisfied Ludwig's illusions of grandeur. He must have a copy of the Château of Versailles itself. So when the island of Herrenworth was offered for sale in 1873—it had been the site of a Benedictine monastery and was just far enough removed from civilization to appeal to the king—he outbid a group of merchants interested in obtaining it for the lumber in its woodlands and thus became the owner. The following year he went incognito to France and spent days roaming around Versailles, taking architectural notes.* He returned to Bavaria pretty well equipped to build a reasonable (though more elaborate) facsimile as tribute to the Grand Monarque. In the

* Frances Gerard, *The Romance of Ludwig II of Bavaria*, London, 1899, p. 148.

new château, called Herrenchiemsee, there were sixteen state rooms containing copies of the paintings of all the great French decorative artists of the eighteenth century, Watteau and Boucher heading the list. Gilding and crystal were everywhere. The Hall of Mirrors contained thirty-three golden lustres that burned 2,500 candles; and Ludwig would spend whole nights gazing at the spectacle, ordering fresh candles to be brought when the old ones had burned to the wick, delighted with the show of seeing the chandeliers lowered to the floor to be serviced and afterwards rising in unison to their normal positions.

Herrenchiemsee was not a comfortable place of habitation. The king's bed was so large that it could have slept a dozen people, the quilt requiring seven years for the seamstresses of Munich to embroider. Ludwig's love of art caused him to suffer the skinning of knees and ankles on the intricate carvings of chair and table legs. He stayed only nine days a year in the palace, arriving at the railroad station on the stroke of midnight on September 29th, whence he was ferried across to the island in a gondola propelled by an oarsman in Venetian costume. The dark hours constituted Ludwig's most active period of the day; and during his sojourn there Herrenchiemsee blazed throughout the night. During the remaining 356 nights of the year it waited for him in patient blackness.

However much he admired the dazzling grandeur of the French, Ludwig was even more captivated by the moody foreboding of the German, which prompted him to begin a fairytale castle at Marienbrücke in 1869. The building was perched atop a series of rugged peaks, commanding a magnificent view up a wild ravine and a gorge unsurpassed for its picturesqueness by any in the Alps, overlooking sublime mountain ranges, with a little village at its feet. Known as Neuschwanstein, it was built mostly of white marble, that gave it an unreal pallor distinguishing it from authentic medieval castles of dark stone. Murals in every room depicted heroes and heroines from the *Nibelungenlied*. The largest interior was the Hall of Singers, measuring 100 by 175 feet, where Ludwig feasted and held solitary court. From his eagle's nest he could look out over a good portion of the world, a special selection of nature that seemed as unsympathetic, desolate, and literally mad as he himself was. In fact, during June of 1886 he was officially pronounced insane, and his uncle assumed the regency. Within a week Ludwig had drowned himself in the Starnberger See, after first disposing of his doctor in like manner, the physician having foolishly accompanied him for a walk unattended. Younger brother Otto succeeded to the throne, and he likewise became incurably insane and had to be supplanted. The Bavarian follies remain as places of pilgrimage for tourists seeking a romantic interpretation of Gallic châteaux or Germanic castles, or simply curious to see in what manner the mad monarch entertained himself in costly, lonely elegance.*

FOLLIES IN AMERICA

THE BUILDING of architectural follies was not restricted by class distinction to grandees, princes, kings, and emperors in the New World as it had been in the Old. In democratic America the field was open to everybody, and many availed themselves of the opportunity to indulge in it. The New Englander, who amassed a fortune in the shipping industry, the Southerner, who became wealthy through agriculture, the showman, who took in great amounts of money on the road, and the parvenu, who got rich practically overnight through banking, merchandising, or other commercial means, erected residences employing any of the various traits of follies. Though few of these republicans' follies were as imposing as those of the dignitaries of Eurasia, some were comparable in size, most were imbued with uniqueness and originality, and a good many—intentionally or not—appeal to our sense of humor, calling forth responses ranging upward from an indulgent chuckle.

It will be recalled that the Father of Our Country liked to dabble in building, mostly at his home, Mount Vernon, which he acquired in 1754. The house at that time was a small story-and-a-half cottage, and George Washington heightened it to a full two stories within the next few years. The building was extended to its present size after the revolution, with the portico added during the 1780's. Washington tried to be on hand during most of these operations, because, he said, the work "goes on better whilst I am present than in my absence"; and whenever the builder failed to show up, the General himself tackled the day's job assisted by his own people. Trying to renovate an irregular little farmhouse into a large, formal mansion presented a number of problems that could hardly be solved successfully; and in its final form Mount Vernon displayed several shortcomings, such as an end of a pediment left dangling over a window, and some of the upper fenestration lighting only the back side of the framework holding up the high coved ceiling of the banqueting hall.

Thomas Jefferson, the ideal American, excelled in many fields Americans regard highly, as a statesman, inventor, collector, archeologist, agriculturist, man of letters,

* For further data on Ludwig's constructions see the recently published: Heinrich Kreisel, *The Castles of Ludwig II of Bavaria*, Darmstadt, n. d.

11. Bladen's Folly, Annapolis, Maryland.
From William Rotch Ware, *The Georgian Period*, Vol. I, New York, 1923.

artist of sorts, and a builder. He once confided to a friend that "putting up and pulling down" was one of his "favorite amusements." It went deeper than that: building and buildings were his periodic passion! From Nimes in southern France he wrote to the Comtesse de Tessé that he found himself "gazing whole hours at the Maison Quarrée, like a lover at his mistress." In Paris, also, he was "violently smitten with the Hôtel de Salm, and used to go to the Tuileries almost daily to look at it." The ancient temple and contemporary residence served respectively as models for his designs of the Virginia State Capitol in Richmond and his own home, Monticello, near Charlottesville, the burdensome upkeep on the latter being the reason for his meeting with financial embarrassment on several occasions.

Mount Vernon and Monticello were but two of the early houses in this country claiming more than ordinary affection from their owners. Some were quite unassuming, such as a little frame house near St. Mary's City, Maryland, called "Clocker's Fancy," which name recalls the original meaning of *folie*. Other early follies of not much architectural interest include Folly Farm near Fairhaven, Connick's Folly near Baden, and The Folly in St. Mary's County, Maryland.*

* Photographs of three of these may be found in the collection of the Historic American Buildings Survey of the Library of Congress, Washington. The last is illustrated in the *Album of American History*, New York, 1944, Vol. I, p. 184.

Maryland also produced at least one sizeable folly. It was begun in Annapolis as the residence of the colonial governor, Thomas Bladen, remembered for the treaty made during his administration with the Six Nations Indians and for rounding out Maryland's western boundary. Bladen was born in America, but was reared and educated in England, and returned to America only after being appointed proprietary governor of the colony in 1742. The gubernatorial house, designed by a Scotch architect named Duff, was well under way when a dispute arose between Bladen and the legislature, which resulted in bringing the work to an abrupt halt. Bladen was relieved of office in 1747, and went back to England. The house remained in an unfinished state for forty years, during which period it came to be referred to as "Bladen's Folly." After the revolution a project was set in motion to resume work on the structure and complete it, not as a residence, however, but as an educational building. Although a new scheme was conceived by Joseph Clark, the architect of the Maryland State House, the final shape of the building in question seems to be mostly a reversion to the original plans, with only minor changes appropriate to its new use as a public building. The structure now is known as McDowell's Hall of St. John's College, a three-storied brick building with a polygonal superstructure topped by a cupola, looking quite innocent of all the fuss that has been raised over it.

2

FOLLIES OF
OLD
MASSACHUSETTS

WHAT MORE fitting place for follies than along the bleak New England coast?

Midway between the towns of Salem, Danvers, and Beverly, in Essex County, Massachusetts, rises a prominence known as "Folly Hill," which now serves as a site for a reservoir. A century ago it was wild and deserted, and became a favorite spot for berry pickers and adventuresome schoolboys, who used to settle themselves in one or the other of a pair of excavations, where—protected from the wind—they would spin yarns about the old manor house that rose above and connected the two depressions. These were cellars in bygone days, and one could be sure that they were well stocked with the best vintage wine.

The house was built for the Honorable William Browne shortly after his marriage in 1733 to fourteen-year-old Mary Burnet, daughter of a former Massachusetts governor. William Browne was ten years her senior.

Mrs. Browne had gone already to her reward in October of 1750, when Browne Hall —as it was then called—was visited by Captain Francis Goelet, and the event recorded in his journal.* The captain was impressed by the fine library, but other rooms lacked furnishings, he said, and the building itself was not quite finished. His host had been much disturbed over the death of his first wife and had neglected to look after the completion of the great house; but at the time of Goelet's visit he was resolved to attend to the matter directly. However, disaster seemed to pursue William Browne: in the earthquake of 1755 the house was so badly shaken apart that it was considered unsafe for occupancy, and consequently was moved to a new site lower down the hill. Here it remained barely six years, when it was divided into three sections, that were carted into Danvers to become three separate buildings. In one of them Colonel Browne

* "Goelet's Journal," *New England Historical and Geneological Register*, Vol. XXIV, 1871, p. 57.

12. Browne's Folly, Essex County.

resided until his death in 1763. One of the others became part of old Berry Tavern, that burned in 1845.

During the second decade of the nineteenth century a boy by the name of Nathaniel used to go to Folly Hill to romp along the seldom-trodden lane and build a miniature dam across the little brook at the base of the hill. Later he described the rise as "a long ridge, rising out of the level country around, like a whale's back out of a calm sea." It was a well conceived simile; but, then, the writer had literary talent. His full name was Nathaniel Hawthorne.

Nathaniel Hawthorne wrote about Folly Hill and what he had heard about the residence of its tenant on two occasions, once on 30 October 1847 (printed in *The American Notebooks*), and again in a letter dated 28 August 1860.* An episode he relates in both writings concerns the adventure of several lads in the abandoned house, told to him by one of them involved in the incident long after it happened. It seems that the place at that time was accessible to whatever idle persons might choose to climb in and explore it. This must have been before its first removal. The following is Hawthorne's later version of the occurrence.

"But there was one closet in the house, which everybody was afraid to enter, it being supposed that an evil spirit—perhaps a domestic Demon of the Browne family—was confined in it. One day, three or four score years ago, some school boys happened to be playing in the deserted chambers, and took it into their heads to develop the secrets of this mysterious closet. With great difficulty and tremor they succeeded in forcing the door. As it flew open, there was a vision of people in garments of antique magnificence. —gentlemen in curled wigs and tarnished gold lace, and ladies in brocade and quaint head-dresses, rushing tumultuously forth and tumbling upon the floor. The urchins took to their heels in huge dismay, but crept back, after a while, and discovered that the apparition was composed of a mighty pile of family portraits."

Hawthorne speaks of Browne Hall as a "pleasure house" built "on a scale of magnificence, which, combined with its airy site and difficult approach, obtained for it and for the entire hill on which it stood the traditionary title of "Browne's Folly." It was a double-storied frame building fashioned on an H plan. The cellars that have been mentioned were under the two wings, there being none under the connecting central hall, which was a great "Assembly or Ball Room," according to Captain Goelet. It was about thirty-three by twenty-three feet in plan; a door was in the center of each of the long sides, facing the sea on the south and looking up an avenue of elms which flanked the driveway connecting with the old Boston Road on the north. Doors in the east and

* "A Stately Pleasure House," *Essex Institute. Historical Collection,* Vol. 31, 1894–95, pp. 207–9.

west walls led into two stairhalls in the wings, with entrances opposite leading to the out-of-doors. When one stood in the center of the ballroom he could look out toward all four points of the compass.

The middle hall was high-ceilinged, which Goelet said represented "a large doom"—one supposes he meant "dome"—and he mentions "a fine Gallery [for musicians] with neat turned Bannesters." Edwin Martin Stone, in his *History of Beverly* (Boston, 1843), adds that the floor of the ballroom was painted in imitation of mosaic and that the musicians' gallery was circular and commodious. The room, he said, provided the setting for many magnificent entertainments.

The wings were 22½ feet across the front ends and 45 feet deep. These contained the well-stocked library, dining room, and chambers, disposed before and to the rear of the stairhalls leading to the second floor level. A separate building to the northwest of the main dwelling housed the negro domestics.

In a portrait (sometimes attributed to John Smibert) of Mary Burnet Browne, owned by descendants living in Virginia, there is depicted a unique authentic representation of Browne Hall. The sketch is very small and quite indistinct, located in the background of the darkened painting. The right hand of the sitter vaguely points in its direction. The house has elongated windows downstairs and attic-sized windows above. The tall, narrow entrance bay and the two end wings are pedimented and pilastered at the corners. The cupola and the small chimneys are seen protruding above the low-pitched roof. The house is shown full front. This view has served as the basis for our own picture of the lumbering old ghost house, quaint and mysterious, as it might look should it suddenly reappear on a gray autumn afternoon.

DEXTER'S FOLLY

THERE is an air of liveliness and humor to our second Massachusetts example that contrasts sharply with the sullen atmosphere hovering about the old house on Folly Hill. Located in Newburyport (also in Essex County) its career was begun as the sober and substantial residence of the merchant Jonathan Jackson, who built it in 1771. The house is a typical late colonial New England type: foursquare and formal, the façade relieved by an elaborate central doorway, and having quoins at the corners; it is prim, precise, and mildly ostentatious, considering its wood construction. Jackson had to dispose of his house because of financial distress; and under the regime of its second owner the place acquired a truly distinctive appearance.

13. *Dexter's Folly, Newburyport.*

The new purchaser was a more adroit businessman than his predecessor, exercising real imagination in everything in which he engaged. His name was Timothy Dexter, but friends and acquaintances alike spoke of him as "Lord" Timothy Dexter, in tribute to his ways and capabilities. He once cornered the whalebone market in New York, Boston, and Salem, and, after fifty days, relinquished the stuff at a profit of seventy-five percent. On another venture he shipped warming pans to the West Indies, where they sold like the proverbial hot cakes for use as dippers and skimmers in sugar mills. Heavy mittens also went to these islands— but there to be transshipped to the Baltic.

Though good-sized, the newly acquired house was too prosaic for the wildly "Lord" Timothy Dexter; and so he set about to make additions, or rather embellishments, dictated by his eccentric interests. As he gloried over having admiration directed toward

14. *Carved figure from garden of Dexter's Folly, thought to represent William Pitt.*

himself, he also delighted in admiring others whom he felt merited the honor; and he assembled the chosen worthies around him in the form of life-size wooden figures stationed about the grounds of his house. These were executed by Joseph Wilson, a young carver of ships' figureheads, and elevated high on columned pedestals or triumphal arches. We are reminded that there have been others in the world who liked statuary so much that they commissioned various amounts of it for private enjoyment, such as Prince Orsini, who is said to have brought back to Italy a number of Turkish prisoners after the battle of Lepanto in 1571, and put them to work in his park at Bomarzo (a village about fifty miles north of Rome) carving out of solid rock gigantic gods and monstrous animals—an elephant, lion, bear, and dragon—and a great gaping chimera mask whose open mouth was the doorway to a cella.* Lord Dexter's taste ran more towards history than to fables and mythology, and the subjects of his wood sculptures included portrayals of the presidents Washington, Jefferson, and Adams, the statesman

* *Harper's Bazaar*, January 1953, pp. /70/–/73/; *ibid.*, July 1958, pp. /70/–/75/.

William Pitt, and others, plus a few allegorical figures, some two dozen in all. Each one was clearly identified by a nameplate, and should any of them fall into disfavor with the temperamental Dexter, away went the label and the name of some other person took its place, often with no change to the statue itself. Our picture of the Dexter premises is based upon an engraving made by John G. Tilton about 1810. It is to be observed that the figures faced the street instead of the house, indicating that their existence was not so much for the personal edification of the owner as for the effect he wished to impose upon passers-by.

The images are reported to have been in good condition when Dexter died. An Indian was first to tumble, and, during the Great September Gale of 1815, all excepting the presidents were cast prostrate on the ground. Afterwards the entire assortment was sold at auction, bringing from fifty cents (for the "Traveling Preacher") to five dollars (for the "Goddess of Fame") apiece. Besides several fragments the only full figure known to be in existence is identified as that of William Pitt. Though vigorously modeled, the pose is stiff and the gesture awkward. The house where these stood is intact, and Wilson's handiwork is represented on it in the wooden eagle still perched atop the cupola. The curving fence has been replaced by a plainer paling.

In their heyday the figures must have made quite a colorful and impressive display. One can imagine them serving as illustrations for history lessons by local pedagogues, as objects of ridicule for the Newburyport ne'er-do-wells, and as indicators of biographical sanction on the part of "Lord" Timothy Dexter himself.

HARRIS' FOLLY

A STONE'S throw away from the scene of the famous Tea Party on the east side of old Boston, at what was formerly the intersection of Hitchinson Street and Cow Lane, now Pearl and High streets, halfway between the present post office and South Station, lies the site of a once grand and imposing house. It might be called appropriately a mansion, so pretentious was it for the period in which it was built. Across the street stood the residence of Jeffrey Richardson, in his day a well-to-do merchant of the city, his three-storied house about equal in size to the Dexter house in Newburyport. But the mansion built facing it towered above the Richardson house like a mother hen over a newly hatched chick.

The larger structure was commissioned by Jonathan Harris about 1800. One thing

15. *Harris' Folly, Boston.*

that contributed to its impressiveness was the location, on a slight rise of ground enclosed by a high masonry wall with a wrought-iron cresting set into the coping, and having urns on the corner piers and gateposts. The house itself had a central pavilion four-stories tall with three-storied wings, the parapets of the wings curving upward at the front to meet the higher walls of the middle section, that was capped by a pediment. There were repetitious rows of windows encircling the building, and a small portico centered on each of the street fronts, sheltering the principal and secondary entrances. The cost of construction of such a great house ruined Harris, who lived in the unfinished building only a few years and then died insolvent, the house becoming known as "Harris' Folly."

Another Boston merchant, by name, Henderson Inches, attempted to occupy a portion of the building; but the neighborhood was not improving, and he moved to the higher-toned atmosphere of Beacon Street overlooking the Common. An effort was made to use the house for an asylum, but this likewise failed. Commerce invaded the locality and Harris' Folly was taken down to be replaced by mercantile buildings, the latter in turn destroyed by the Great Fire of 1872.

Fate stamps the seal of disapproval upon certain buildings, from which there is no redress. The Browne house on Folly Hill is one: moved down the hillside and later divided up and taken into town, it was dogged by ill luck wherever it went. The Harris house in Boston stood its ground, but no matter what efforts were made to convert it to some worthwhile use, it was never found suitable for anything. Doomed from the beginning, such buildings are inherent follies.

3

FOLLIES OF
THE EARLY
REPUBLIC IN
PENNSYLVANIA

DURING the days of the early republic, Philadelphia was the center of taste and elegance in the United States. The city was our first capital and its architecture lived up to this distinction. Here was gathered together a number of wealthy financiers, whose homes did justice, and—as we shall see—sometimes even injustice, to their fortunes.

George Washington and his family resided in one of these houses throughout his tenure as president in the Pennsylvania city. Rented for the executive mansion in 1790, Washington himself proclaimed it "the best single house in the city." A three-and-a-half-story brick house at Sixth and Market streets, it had been constructed for Richard Penn, and, at this time, was owned by Robert Morris, former Minister of Finance and Marine, currently a senator from Pennsylvania, who also owned, and occupied, the adjoining house. These residences were in the Georgian or colonial style of their day, having walls of red brick relieved by carved wood trim. Robert Morris wanted something more pretentious, distinctive, and continental than what he had for his domestic setting; so, in 1791, he purchased the entire block bounded by Chestnut and Walnut, Seventh and Eighth streets for £10,000 and commissioned the French architect, Major Pierre Charles l'Enfant, to provide him with a design that would be the most outstanding in America. The architect, it will be remembered, was, during this period, drafting the layout for the new capital city of Washington in the District of Columbia.

L'Enfant conceived a mansion in the French Baroque manner (a type already rather passé in France, though in time to be revived with enthusiasm under Napoleon III, during the era designated the Second Empire), with curved walls, elaborate porticoes at the doors and meticulous relief work around the windows; and crowning the edifice was a steeply pitched Mansard roof—the first in America, not to be deprived of its uniqueness until the Cabildo in New Orleans acquired one half a century later. The Morris house was made to face Chestnut Street, and alternative accounts relate of its

16. Morris' Folly, Philadelphia.

being built entirely of pale-blue marble or of a combination of marble and brick. It must have measured eighty by one hundred feet across the façade and probably ran back forty to sixty feet.

Robert Morris was spurred on to new ventures as his house slowly took shape. It was, he confessed, even "a much more magnificent house than I ever intended to have built," He entered into land speculations with John Nicholson and James Greenleaf, only to be caught up in a changing tide of economics which undermined his wealth; and with this unfortunate occurrence work on the marble house came to a halt. Up to this time the citizenry of the Friendly City had referred to it as the "Marble Palace," but now it became known as "Morris' Folly." The unfinished structure was sold about the turn of the century to satisfy Morris' creditors, and afterwards, although some attempt was made to continue building operations for some years, finally the job was given up as impracticable, and the existing construction razed.

A representation of the Morris place, entitled, "An Unfinished House, in Chestnut Street," survives among William Birch's famous views of *The City of Philadelphia... as it Appeared in the Year 1800,* and another in a rendering by William Strickland. The accompanying illustration is based upon the former view. Some of the sculpture from the house went into Benjamin Henry Latrobe's Chestnut Street Theater,[*] and several carved marble panels and column capitals fashioned for it were for many years displayed at the Conshohocken quarry.

Robert Morris paid out over £6,000 on the Marble Palace, the architect receiving $9,037.13 for his services. The building being so ample it seems unlikely Morris ever expected to occupy it all himself. Indeed Strickland refers to it as a four-dwelling "Republican Abode,"[†] which coincides with the form of the house as pictured, displaying four separate entrances. The glazed bird-cage skylights on the roof would indicate the presence of stair wells beneath. There being only two showing, however, the house may have been intended only as a duplex originally, and was subdivided after Morris' regime, making it into more restricted units. By this time the seat of the national government had been transferred to the banks of the Potomac, and perhaps affluent tenants were more difficult to find.

In Pennsylvania there is another "Morris' Folly," or rather "Maris' Folly," having a variation in the spelling of the proper name. The latter is a house on the outskirts of New Hope, built by William Maris about 1816 and designated by the builder "Cintra,"

[*] Thompson Westcott, *The Historic Mansions and Buildings of Philadelphia*, Philadelphia, /1877/, p. 364.
[†] Communication from Carl W. Dreppard, 24 December 1953.

after the old palace of the Moors and later native kings of Portugal, which building impressed Maris upon visiting it in 1814, just as it impressed Lord Byron, who spoke of it as "Cintra's glorious Eden" in *Childe Harold.* No credence can be put in the legend that the Bucks County house is a copy of the Portuguese villa, to which it bears not the slightest resemblance. Its plan seems to have been derived from that of William Thornton's Octagon (1798) at 1741 New York Avenue in Washington, substituting a polygonal for the circular entrance hall at the angle of the two wings of the building. The application of "Maris' Folly" to Cintra may have been suggested by the better-known folly in Philadelphia, some confusion resulting from the accidental similarities in the builders' surnames.*

PICNIC HOUSE

MARY ELIZABETH was the apple of her father's eye, and while she was still a young girl the rich William Croghan built for his daughter a pavilion on Black Horse Hill near their home in Pittsburgh. This was about 1830. Situated on a high rise of ground the pavilion commanded a wide vista on all sides. It was an ideal site. The building contained an elaborate ballroom and three smaller rooms reserved for Mary Elizabeth's parties when she grew up, and it was given the festive name of "Picnic House." No expense was spared in decorating the interiors. Deep fretwork and foliated reliefs ornamented the ceiling, anthemion and acanthus motifs formed a continuous design in the frieze, coupled Corinthian columns and pilasters with decorated capitals marched in stately procession around the perimeter of the ballroom, in the center of which was hung one of the most magnificent crystal chandeliers thus far imported to America, and all was reflected and reduplicated in the mirrors on the walls and in the polished floor. It was an enchanting spectacle giving promise of many joyous occasions the future held in store.

But love stepped in and changed the course of hoped-for events.

While Mary Elizabeth was away at boarding school she met Captain Edward Wyndham Harrington Schenley of the British army, a veteran of the Battle of Waterloo over three times her age, whom she found dashing and attractive, and turned a sympathetic ear to his proposal of elopement. It was a great scandal, of course, not so much because

---

* Illustrations, including a plan of the New Hope house, are included in an article by Hannah Coryell Anderson, "Cintra," *American Magazine of Art,* June 1917, pp. 310–13.

17. Ballroom of Picnic House, Pittsburgh.

18. Picnic House or Croghan's Folly.

of the difference in their years as because the bride was an American heiress allying herself with one considered an adventurer and a foreigner. It is said that after Mary Elizabeth Croghan's marriage the Pennsylvania legislature attempted to pass a law prohibiting her husband from touching a penny of her money.*

Captain Schenley took his young bride to live in England. The loss was more than William Croghan could bear, and to induce her to return to this country he set about to enlarge the pavilion on Black Horse Hill. A new mass several times the size of the original structure was added to Picnic House, providing amply for family and servants, the old and new parts tied together by a lengthy open gallery along one side; and stables and kennels were built for the horses and hounds belonging to a sporting Britisher's household. During the 1840's the Schenleys returned and took up residence in the big house. The children (there were to be nine altogether) romped up and down the long gallery and out over the hill. Picnic House at last seemed to serve the purpose for which it was erected. Its life as such, however, was short-lived, because after a few years the Schenleys went back to England, leaving the house quiet and deserted, except for a lone caretaker. Picnic House had become a folly for the second time.

Shadows began to gather over the great pile. Dust collected. Paint started to peel and the plaster to drop from the ornate ceilings. The boards of the porch began to rot away. After the course of a century the house became rather shabby looking. But while the house had deteriorated, the land, due to its location, had increased in value. Finally

* *Life* magazine, June 1945, p. 125.

the inevitable happened. The Schenley descendants in England sold the property for a housing project. The house was demolished, but the ballroom of Picnic House was saved, reinstalled in the Cathedral of Learning at the University of Pittsburgh, set up as near to its original form as the structure of the university tower would permit, becoming one of the show places of the institution.

4

ARCHAISMS

WHAT GREATER folly could modern man perpetrate than to pattern his home after an ancient Greek temple or medieval gothic cathedral? Yet during the eighteenth and nineteenth centuries this occurred so frequently that the practice became commonplace; and through our being constantly confronted with the results, the phenomenon has ceased to strike us as being remarkable. Actually, it is all the more noteworthy for having become so universal.

It was inevitable, in Europe during the eighteenth century, when the Renaissance enthusiasm over things Roman had begun to wear thin, and archeologists, through excavation, began to open up new fields of exploration (and exploitation) among the ruins of ancient Greece, that designers and artists should turn for inspiration to the same source which had prompted much of the grandeur that had been old Rome itself. Authentic designs of Greek buildings were made available in England through the publication of Stuart and Revett's *The Antiquities of Athens,* four volumes of finely delineated plates, appearing between 1762 and 1816, with a supplement published in 1830. The first pure Greek building of this time is believed to have been the Doric garden temple on Lord Lyttelton's estate at Hagley, near Birmingham, built by one of the authors of *The Antiquities,* James Stuart, in 1758. Thus, the initial monument of the Greek Revival—a garden temple—started the movement off in line with the accepted folly tradition.

Introduced into the United States by Benjamin Henry Latrobe in 1799, the Greek Revival mode became more popular in the New World than it ever had been in Europe, partly due to its being linked up with the ideal of freedom maintained by the Greek city-states. The Greek Revival assumed the status of the American national architectural style during the middle decades of the 1800's. In a sense every building cast in the mold of former ages is a folly, and there are many houses in the Greek manner to which the term "folly" specifically has been attached. One is the Kelley house built a short

19. *Pitts' Folly, near Uniontown, Alabama.*

distance outside Columbus, Ohio, about 1839. A more imposing contemporary example is "Manning's Folly" near Stateburg, South Carolina. Another, chosen for discussion below, is "Pitts' Folly," located in the Black Belt of the Deep South.

Constructed near Uniontown, Alabama, in 1852–53, the Phillip Henry Pitts house sports pretentious, colossal Doric colonnades, pseudo-temple style, on two sides. The pedimented roof fails to cover the entire structure, which shortcoming is compensated for by an additional flat roof masked by a parapet over the deep entablature on the north front of the building. Inside the range of columns a cantilevered gallery calls attention to the second-floor level, which is something nonexisting among the original Hellenic temple archetypes. The impressiveness of the architecture is a direct carry-over from that of old Virginia, from which state Henry Pitts had emigrated. The residence appeared so incongruous to this locale—as though having wandered off and gotten lost in the Alabama woodlands—that it is little wonder the simple-minded neighbors dwelling in log cabins soon attached to it the derisive epithet by which it is known. The builder assessed his house as having cost him $170,000. B. F. Parsons of Marion was the architect.*

The proportions of the house are heavy, the portico forms being more sympathetic to stone construction than to wood, of which less durable material they are fashioned. The alignment of nine columns constitutes the entrance façade of the house. The front doorway, recessed behind a pair of smaller supports matching the great ones, opens into a central transverse hall. An unusual feature inside is a secret staircase, the existence of which is not suspected from the exterior. The house contains much of its original furnishings; and whatever its shortcomings may be, it has not been a folly in the sense that it has not served its intended purpose. Unlike Picnic House, for instance, the Alabama residence has remained in the possession and use of the family which built it for more than a century, and was carefully restored in 1948.

WEDDING-CAKE HOUSE

ON THE estate with the Doric garden temple at Hagley, the same owner erected, at the same time, a gothic ruin for a keeper's lodge. The medieval-style structure was not the first revival of its kind in England. As a matter of fact, the gothic being native to Britain, there was a trickle of it surviving and being used throughout the Renais-

* Ralph Hammond, *Ante-Bellum Mansions of Alabama*, New York, 1951, p. 138.

sance period: even that great classicist, Sir Christopher Wren, architect of Saint Paul's Cathedral, designed in gothic in Oxford and in seven London parish churches. But the revival of gothic in England had its real inception in the remodeling and enlarging of "Strawberry Hill" for Horace Walpole in the middle of the eighteenth century. The term "gothic" (meaning "barbaric") was a reproach that had been leveled against late medieval architecture by thoroughgoing advocates of the classic, but Walpole's use of it reinstated its social standing, so to speak. The most ambitious domestic establishment to be built in the new gothic taste was "Fonthill Abbey," William Beckford's sumptuous country seat, designed and constructed by James Wyatt during the 1790's and early 1800's. An imposing staircase in the great entrance hall led up to an octagon in the central tower, having a ceiling height of almost 128 feet, the tower itself rising about twice that height from the ground upward.* The shoddy building methods employed (the tower collapsed early in 1800, and had to be rebuilt) attest to the sham quality of much of this variety of romantic building. One of the most famous of Gothic Revival houses in England (because of its builder) was Sir Walter Scott's "Abbotsford," sponsored by the author of the Waverly novels in 1812. As with the Greek so with the Gothic Revival: proper forms for modern buildings were made available through illustrated publications, such as the books of Batty Langley in the mid eighteenth century, and of Augustus Welby Pugin (the designer of the Houses of Parliament) during the 1830's and 1840's.

National pride was not a factor favoring the gothic in the United States, as it had been in Europe, especially in England; but the persisting tendency to imitate the Mother Country afforded the vogue support enough. Introduced into America by Latrobe, the same architect who instituted the Greek Revival, and in the same year (1799), houses here soon came to be built in the "castellated" and in the English Tudor or "pointed" styles, the difference between them being that between extensive baronial manors on the one hand and of smaller cottages with steeply pitched roofs on the other. Regardless of size, both types exhibited an assortment of gables, bay windows, pinnacles, tracery, and chimney stacks, compared to which conceits the Greek Revival seemed quite restrained, though both were derivative. Certain American architects and miscellaneous aesthetes enjoyed exercising their imaginations in the new idiom, allowing their pencils to go flying off into wild flights of fancy in the designs that developed on their drawing boards. There was, moreover, a concise philosophy accompanying the gothic movement, centering around a picturesque approach to architecture, that is, considering the house as having picture value in the natural landscape, rather than as remaining a self-con-

* H. A. N. Brockman, "Fonthill Abbey," *Architectural Review*, June 1944, pp. 149–56.

20. Wedding-Cake House, Kennebunk, Maine.

tained unit that could be placed anywhere, as was the case with most Greek Revival houses. The Gothic Revival, theoretically, was part of its outdoor environment, in its irregular outlines, lacey decorations, and harmonious polychromy. Its appeal was in large measure due to its identification with its setting.

The rugged forests, jagged peaks, and deep ravines of the Hudson River country rendered this region an especially favorite haunt of romantic building, largely inspired by the nostalgic legends of Washington Irving and his own imitation Dutch farmhouse, "Sunnyside" (the counterpart of Scott's "Abbotsford"), having crow-stepped gables and gothic porches dating from the 1830's. One of the great houses in this vicinity was Philip Paulding's "Lyndhurst," perched atop a hill near Tarrytown, which has been described by a contemporary observer as resembling "a Gothic monastery, with towers, turrets and trellises; minarets, mosaics, and mouse-holes; archways, armories, and air-holes; peaked windows and pinnacled roofs, and many other fantastics too tedious to enumerate, the whole constituting an edifice of gigantic size, with no room in it; great cost and little comfort, which, if I mistake not, will one of these days be designated as *Paulding's Folly*."* Twenty years after these lines were written the house was enlarged! Some miles north of Lyndhurst, on an island in the Hudson near Barrytown, John Church Cruger built a mock ruin in the form of a series of rustic arches pretending to be the remains of the nave of a crumbling cathedral.†

Even staid New England gave in to its emotions in architecture during the nineteenth century as readily as it had given in to its sentiments in religion some generations earlier, with comparably drastic results, yet leaving behind more tangible monuments during the later phase than was left by the witchhunt Reign of Terror. Some of the constructions were not built from the ground up but were only altered in the new style. An example is a house situated about a mile northeast of Kennebunk, Maine, originally a symmetrical, four-square brick house of sober mien, onto which an owner at mid century lavished his whimsy for archaic ornamentation.

Locally the tale is told that a sea captain was in the midst of celebrating his nuptials when news was brought of a nearby disaster at sea. Answering the call to duty, so the story continues, his absence was of longer duration than he had anticipated, so long, in fact, that the bride was deprived of the ceremonial of the cutting of the wedding cake —coveted by every new wife as the first privilege allowed her following the tying of the marriage knot, whereby she assumes the prerogative of managing every matter of joint concern from then on. Anyway, to appease the lady for the misadventure, when the

* *The Diary of Philip Hone, 1828–1851*, New York, 1927, Vol. II, p. 550.
† Pictured in Croswell Bowen, *The Hudson*, New York, 1941, p. /47/.

captain returned he directed frosting to be applied to their domicile, which, with its at-
tenuated corner buttresses, slender spires, fancy arches, pendants, crockets, finials, and
trefoil perforations, took on the appearance of the unaccounted-for wedding cake. Even
the barn attached to the rear of the house and the fence in front were sprinkled with
the same sugary motifs. The effect was a tour de force, a monumental patisserie, the
triumph of the bakeoven over the architecture of the whole house!

5

ORIENTAL

EXOTICISMS

BY THE second quarter of the nineteenth century America had become not only a haven for European malcontents but a land of golden opportunity for the commercially enterprising, the earlier expectation of extracting gold effortless from the native population having run its course. One of the most colorful personalities to come to America on the newer venture was Mrs. Frances (Thomas Anthony) Trollope, the daughter of a clergyman, wife of a neurotic barrister of depleted circumstances, and mother of five children, three of whom accompanied her on her quest. Mrs. Trollope had been persuaded by the aging Lafayette and a juvenile, wealthy, and well-meaning suffragette, named Frances Wright, to attempt to replenish the family's finances on the American frontier. She accompanied Miss Wright to the mouth of the Mississippi River and proceeded up as far as Nashoba, the latter's idealistic but poorly equipped colony of emancipated negroes in Tennessee. Also in the party was an artist and political refugee, M. Auguste Hervieu, who was expected to remain with Miss Wright to impart a knowledge of art to her colonists, but who absconded from this assignment on the day they arrived at Nashoba, and, linking fortunes with Mrs. Trollope, continued with her to Cincinnati. Mrs. Trollope thus disembarked on 10 February 1828 at her destination, a rude and virile town, exacting if not cultivated, and prudish if not refined: she had neglected to bring letters of introduction to influential people who might have been of assistance to her; she traveled without husband (an unpardonable breach!); in the company of a French artist (still worse!!!); and she was here on a strange undertaking, the means (if not the object) of which was most irregular.

Mrs. Trollope had been preceded in this locale by another Britisher, William Bullock, Esq., who had proclaimed the house and estate of Thomas D. Carneal, across the Ohio River from Cincinnati, to be the finest he had seen in his travels along the Mississippi and its tributaries, and had become the purchaser of the property in 1827, with the

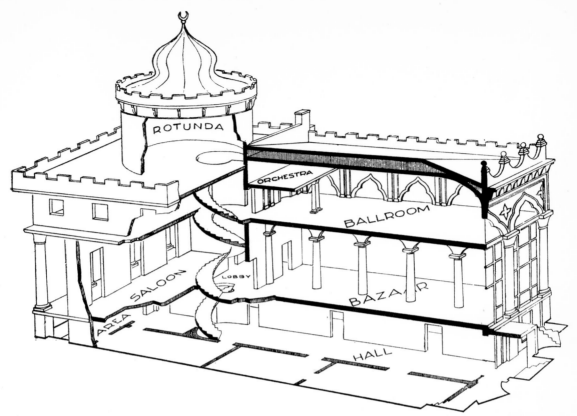

21. Perspective section of Mrs. Trollope's bazaar, Cincinnati. Conjectural reconstruction.

intent of making a model rural town of it. Bullock had been the former proprietor of
Egyptian Hall, a museum in Piccadilly, London, styled after antique architecture along
the Nile.* Shortly after her arrival in Cincinnati Mrs. Trollope called on Mr. Bullock;
and if the image of Egyptian Hall were not in her mind before the visit we can be certain that it was afterwards. She was going to erect a building for a bazaar modeled on
Mr. Bullock's museum. The design would be so unusual that it would stand out in sharp
contrast to the normal run of Cincinnati buildings, where hardly a church steeple broke
the sober skyline formed by the square wooden blocks sheltering the city's twenty thousand inhabitants; and inside the architectural wonder the townspeople and backwoods-
men would have the opportunity of purchasing rare and beautiful—sometimes even
useful—objects, at some profit to Mrs. Trollope, of course. Perhaps, even, she could
introduce these rustic folk to the polite English custom of drinking tea at five o'clock
every afternoon, which would add greatly to her anticipated triumph in the interest of
culture.

Mrs. Trollope's spouse and eldest son arrived in Cincinnati late in November of 1828,
and on the first day of the following January a narrow, though deep, lot was purchased
for a building site on the river side of Third Street near Broadway. Mr. Seneca Palmer, a
resident architect of "classical taste in architecture," was commissioned to draw the
plans and superintend the erection of the edifice. In February Thomas Anthony Trol-

* The author's "The Egyptian Hall and Mrs. Trollope's Bazaar," *Magazine of Art,* March 1950,
pp. 94–99, 112.

lope departed for England to procure ten thousand dollars' worth of goods in London to stock the bazaar.

By the beginning of November, 1829, the bazaar presented some tangible form and was given a 1,400-word review in the *Cincinnati Chronicle and Literary Gazette,* and a description of almost equal length in the contemporary *City Directory.* Both begin by describing the basement, that contained an "Exchange Coffee House," a bar, and other shops "divided by a hall sixty feet long, terminating at the foot of the grand circular staircase ascending to the terrace." The staircase was the means of vertical communication throughout the building, mounting all the way up to the roof level.

The *Directory* extols the "splendid compartment" on the main floor that "gives *title,* if not character, to the building. Here is to be held THE BAZAAR, where it is presumable, every useful and useless article, in dress, in stationery, in light and ornamental household furniture, chinas and more pellucid porcelain, with every gew-gaw that can contribute to the splendor and attractiveness of the exhibition, from the sparkling necklace of 'Lady fair' to the Exquisite's *safety chain,* will be displayed and vended.

"In the rear of the BAZAAR is an elegant SALOON," continues the *Directory,* "where *Ices* and other refreshments will lend their allurements to the fascinations of architectural novelty. This Saloon opens to a spacious BALCONY, which in its turn, conducts to an EXHIBITION GALLERY, that is at present occupied by *Mr. Hervieu's* superb picture of LAFAYETTE'S *landing at* CINCINNATI." The *Chronicle* mentions that a lobby, "through which passes the great circular stair-case, leading to the rotunda and the Ball-room," separates the bazaar proper from the saloon, and that the balcony is formed by "Egyptian columns." It also states that the exhibition gallery was housed in a separate building.

The ballroom over the bazaar was the *pièce de résistance* of the building. "The large arabesque windows in front, the lofty walls, and arched ceiling give a fine effect to this apartment. Across the south end of this room and immediately over the entrance to it, is an elegant orchestra, supported by four Corinthian columns." The journal mentions that the decorations are by M. Hervieu: "In ornamenting this room the object of the artist has been to follow as closely as possible the style of the Alhambra, the celebrated palace of the Moorish kings in Granada. The architecture is a mixture of Saracenic and Gothic; the ornaments are painted to imitate mosaic, and the roof represents masses of granite decorated at intervals by mosaic designs of a great variety of objects, and by accurate imitations of the brilliantly coloured tiles so much used in the Alhambra. The sides of the room represent a double row of marble pilasters, between which are windows, corresponding with those in the front, richly draped with crimson curtains,

22. *Sketch of Trollope's bazaar.*
From Charles Frederic Goss,
Cincinnati, the Queen City,
Vol. I, Chicago, 1912.

"TROLLOPE'S FOLLY"
Mrs. Trollope's Bazaar in Cincinnati.
Erected 1828-9; demolished 1881.

through which a variety of Spanish scenery is seen. The perspective in these picturesque views is remarkably fine, and does much credit to the artist." The *Directory* states that behind the ballroom was a second saloon "assigned to the accommodation of gentlemen's parties, where the *beau-monde* may regale themselves when, and how they list."

The crowning glory of the bazaar was the cylindrical superstructure, described in the *Chronicle* as "a rotunda twenty-eight feet in diameter and eighteen feet in height to the cornice, or twenty-four to the apex of the curvilinear roof, on which is to be placed as an ornament a large Turkish crescent.

"The walls of this rotunda will receive about 1500 feet of canvas, which is to be decorated for panoramic exhibition by the pencil of Mr. Hervieu. The gothic battlements surrounding its base, and forming the summit of its entablature, afford protection to a fine promenade, commanding an extensive view of the city and surrounding country." The panorama was a popular and lucrative outlet for the early-nineteenth-century painter's craft, and Mrs. Trollope's sense of the dramatic was not to miss its possibilities atop her repository of culture.

The principal façade did justice to the exotic interior. The *Chronicle* gives the height from the basement floor to the top of the crenelations as fifty-two feet; and from the base of the columns to the top of the crescent measured eighty-five feet. The street front was "formed of three large Arabesque windows with arches, supported by four Moorish stone pilasters with capitals, over which are inserted large and beautifully wrought free stone ornaments." It presented "a rich and tasty compound of ancient and modern architecture, but varying so much from the former, as to possess strong claims to originality." We are informed that the inspiration for this elevation was taken "in part from the Mosquee of St. Athanase, in Egypt." The dedication of a mosque to a Christian saint is most unusual, but perhaps the statement refers to an early church consecrated to Saint Athanasius, Archbishop of Alexandria, later appropriated by the Moslems. The four pilasters are hardly "Moorish"; they probably matched the columns of a rear portico "modeled after those in the temple of Apollinopolis at Etfou, as exhibited in Denon's Egypt." The bell-form capitals of the temple columns at Edfu were a familiar model; and it is worth noting that Denon's two-volume work, *Voyages dans la Basse et la Haute Egypte,* published in London in 1809, supplied details for the front of William Bullock's Egyptian Hall. Perhaps the same copies were used in designing both the Piccadilly museum and Cincinnati bazaar.

Luck seems to have been against Mrs. Trollope from the beginning. Her management of the bazaar was short-lived. First the gas mains that had been installed for illuminating the building began to leak, and oil lamps had to be substituted. Then she became seriously ill with malaria; and while she was incapacitated the ten thousand dollar consignment of goods was bartered to small shopkeepers and her personal property suffered a similar disposition. Mrs. Trollope was obliged to recuperate surrounded by her troupe in borrowed quarters. She made a stab at selling products of domestic manufacture, exhibiting M. Hervieu's paintings and offering evenings of musical and dramatic entertainment in the ballroom, the last with the help of Mr. Alexander Drake, "a strolling manager" from the west of England, who "some years before had brought to this country a large family of children, all educated to sing, dance, fight combats, paint scenes, play the fiddle, and everything else."* Conspicuous in these affairs was Mrs. Drake. But the audience was small, and, as the English comedian said, it was "a wonder there were any there at all, her [Mrs. Trollope's] philosophical mode of going to heaven being objectionable to a large portion of the American population."

Soon the building went under the sheriff's hammer at auction. Mrs. Trollope sent her son Henry back to England early in 1830 and arranged for her daughters, M. Hervieu, and herself to follow in March. Before quitting America the party visited Wheeling,

* Joe Cowell, *Thirty Years Passed Among the Players in England and America*, New York, 1844, Vol. II, p. 87.

Baltimore, Washington, Philadelphia, New York, and Niagara Falls, for the express purpose of allowing Frances Trollope to gather material for the proposed book that was to be the saving of the family. M. Hervieu's gift for portraiture made these final rambles financially possible. They arrived home in the late summer of 1831; and in March of the following year appeared *The Domestic Manners of the Americans,* which made its authoress the sensation of the hour. The thousand pounds received for the book did much to soothe the bitterness of having lost an estimated twenty to twenty-five thousand dollars in the States, and besides this remuneration the book secured the writer sufficient prestige to warrant the success of whatever subsequent works she might care to have published.

In Cincinnati the bazaar became known as "Trollope's Folly." Its sponsor had hoped that it might become a church after it had failed to become a commercial success—at least giving the Cincinnatians religion if not refinement of taste—but instead it was first occupied by the Ohio Mechanics' Institute. When Mrs. Trollope's youngest son visited Ohio in 1861–62 "It had become a 'Physico-medical Institute'...under the dominion of a quack doctor on one side and a college of rights-of-women female medical professors on the other." Finally, so it is rumored, it descended to serving as a house of ill-repute prior to its demolition in 1881. One proprietor summed up general sentiments when he said: "I believe, sir, no man or woman ever made a dollar in that building; and as for rent, I don't even expect it." The significance of the bazaar was outside the ken of utilitarian architecture; it was for half a century a monument to repeated failures, and after that a memory to the futility of ambitious enterprise.

IRANISTAN

PHINEAS Taylor Barnum was a born showman. But he had no interest in producing shows that might be considered high types of art. Production itself was his objective —quantitative production, production for the masses. "A sucker is born every minute" was his resolute motto; and the sucker was a person seeking entertainment, who could be lured into the showman's den. Not culture, not beauty, and not learning was what the public wanted, but entertainment!—to be dazzled, amused, and even deceived— anything, so long as it was a "good" show. P. T. Barnum gave them what they wanted, graciously accepting their coin of admission for the services rendered. He saw to it that they got a "good" show, and he made money in the process.

23. *A close-up view of Iranistan,
Bridgeport, Connecticut.*
From *The Life of P. T. Barnum
Written by Himself*, New York,
1888.

    Barnum's true character was revealed in the home he built for himself as a young
man (not yet forty) at Bridgeport, Connecticut. It was ornate and exotic; and the proud
owner capitalized on its unusual appearance for his own ends. Built within eyeshot of
the New York and New Haven Railroad, at that time the busiest line in America, the
picturesque and colorful villa offered a none-too-subtle reminder to westbound passengers to visit Barnum's famous American Museum in New York City, where there were
more, and more fascinating, oddities to inspect at closer range.

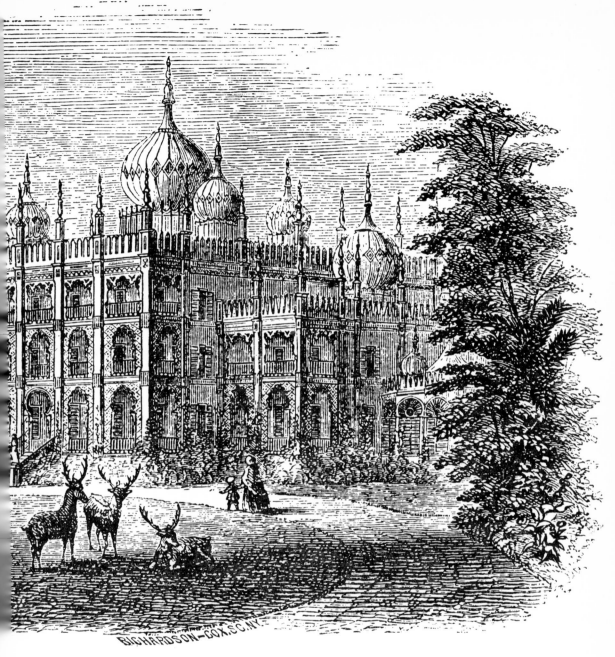

RICHARDSON-COX.SC.N.Y.

ANISTAN.

The house was christened "Iranistan," and a waggish New York editor divided the name into four syllables, "I-ran-i-stan," and said that Barnum, in settling down, was declaring, "I ran a long time before I could stan'!" But Barnum, who never liked for anyone—other than himself—to perpetrate a pointed aphorism, declared that this was not true. "Literally," he announced quite gravely, "the name signifies, 'Eastern Country Place,' or, more poetically, 'oriental villa.'"*

* *Life of P. T. Barnum Written by Himself*, Buffalo, 1888, p. 97.

An "Oriental" villa the house attempted to be, with polychromed bulbous domes, minarets, spires, and tracery verandahs. The inspiration for the house had come to Barnum while touring abroad with his diminutive companion and prize exhibit, "General" Tom Thumb. After successful and lucrative appearances in France and Belgium, they returned to England where levees were given for the "wealth and fashion" of London to meet the American midget, held in Egyptian Hall, Piccadilly (the very building that had served as archetype for Mrs. Trollope's bazaar in Cincinnati). Barnum took the opportunity to visit Brighton and became enchanted with the Indian-style pavilion erected by George IV. He therefore determined—so he said—to duplicate the building, and "engaged a London architect to furnish...a set of drawings after the general plan of the Pavilion." He purchased a seventeen-acre tract near Bridgeport, and the plans supposedly brought from London were entrusted to "a competent architect and builder," sparing "neither time nor expense in erecting a comfortable, convenient and tasteful residence." The work was executed while the client went off on another tour with the "General."

The myths centering around his house no doubt pleased Barnum as much, or more, than any other aspect having to do with the place; and, as with his other enterprises, he spared neither trouble nor expense to circulate as many as possible. Usually he got away with these inventions. Once he was caught up with. At this point I must confide in the reader that the designs of Iranistan really originated on the drawing boards of a young New York architect by the name of Leopold Eidlitz and that they were ordered through an agent. Eidlitz had a flair for Oriental forms and later designed a number of metropolitan synagogues in this idiom. He had nothing to do with the actual construction of the house, in fact never saw it in process of building. Some time after its completion, however, he went out to Bridgeport to inspect the building. The actualization of his drawings struck him as something beyond his wildest dream. "In the same spirit of mischief which had inspired the design," so the story goes, "he rang the doorbell, which was answered by the showman in person." The visitor professed considerable admiration for the edifice, and inquired the source of the design. It was the result of a cosmopolitan competition, he was told, that had cost the owner a goodly ten thousand dollars. " 'No it didn't,' retorted the actual designer, whereto the showman with a presence of mind which at once explained and justified his success in humbug, softly queried, 'Is your name Eidlitz?' "*

The housewarming was on 14 November 1848, attended by one thousand invited

* Montgomery Schuyler, "A Great American Architect: Leopold Eidlitz," *Architectural Record*, September 1908, pp. 169–70.

24. *Iranistan.*

guests. It was a motley gathering inasmuch as the host knew and associated with people from all walks of life. Rich and poor alike found much to marvel at in the new house. A popular contemporary magazine described the building as being of "the Byzantine, Moorish, and Turkish styles of architecture." Undoubtedly so designated to the reporter interviewing the owner. The description continues in this manner:

"Its entire front is 124 feet, the wings being thrown off irregularly, with domed conservatories at each extremity; the main building consists of three stories, each having broad piazzas supported by colonnades of graceful pillars, surmounted by minarets of the most elegant appearance. About the center of the great hall springs a noble winding staircase, with a carved balustrade of black walnut, which, gradually contracting, winds to the observatory in the central dome; the niches of the staircase are embellished with marble statuary, imported from Florence; opposite to the base of the staircase, large sliding doors open into a very beautiful drawing-room, the walls of which are covered with a rich fresco paper, the principal panels of which represent the four seasons; the ceiling is of rich arabesque mouldings of white and gold; the mantels, of Italian statuary marble; a royal Wilton carpet, of gorgeous pattern, covers the floor; the furniture is of rich rosewood; the curtains, drapery, statuary, mantel ornaments, etc., are of unique elegance; while the pier glasses, at each end, and the large folding-doors opening into the hall and dining-room, of plate-mirror panels on each side, apparently multiply infinitely this beautiful section of the house.

"The dining-room is an elegant square apartment; the walls are painted in dark English oak, the rich panels of which represent the three fine arts, Music, Painting and Poetry; the ceiling has richly gilded mouldings; the furniture is of black walnut, including a cabinet of rare and beautiful porcelain, among which is a harlequin dessert-service, every piece of a different pattern, lettered with the intials, P. T. B."*

The effect was mostly what Barnum desired. One notes the use of the adjective "rich" applied four times in the foregoing description, together with the adverb "richly," and also such high-sounding—though descriptively meaningless—words as "elegant," "gorgeous," and "beautiful." We gather from the written and pictorial evidence that has come down to us that the plan was that of a typical medium-to-large-sized American country house, with the stairhall in the center, and rooms and wings disposed right and left. Upon this indigenous shell was overspread a wealth of Oriental finery having little to do with the function of the structure it obscured. The central dome afforded light to the circular staircase; but this could have been accomplished more adequately by a simple glazed cupola. Only in the individual features of the outer dress do we

* *Gleason's Pictorial Drawing-Room Companion*, 1851, p. 57.

find resemblances to the pavilion at Brighton: in similar motifs at the entasis of the domes, crenelations like those on the façade toward the Steine, with minarets applied like gothic pinnacles; lattices enframe the keyhole openings in the porches; and concave conical roofs on the terminal conservatories at Iranistan echo the roof forms of the huge Banqueting Room and Music Room at Brighton. The interpretation of Mughal architecture in the Connecticut villa is revealingly provincial.

There is some discrepancy among the contemporary representations of Iranistan. A front elevation view in *Gleason's Pictorial Drawing-Room Companion* for 1851 shows it to have a central mass five bays across, with attached wings three bays wide, whereas the three-quarter view of the house (here illustrated) in *The Life of P. T. Barnum* of 1855 indicates that the wings were only two bays wide. Another three-quarter view (showing the right instead of the left flank), a lithograph by Sarony & Major of New York, confirms the three-bayed wings; and another front elevation in the 1888 edition of the autobiography likewise accords with the *Gleason's* view, perhaps taken from it, the house at that time being no longer in existence. The odd version, in the first *Life*, one supposes to have been misinterpreted by the engraver, working probably from a drawing made on the spot by a camera lucida. The subsidiary buildings were grouped informally at the back of the villa. One of the dependencies bore a slight resemblance to a mosque. The stables (behind the right wing of the house) featured square pavilions with sagging hipped roofs.

The knowledgeable critics of his day bombarded Barnum's home with sharp reproach. The best known of these was Andrew Jackson Downing, the "Hudson-River aesthete." In Downing's book, *The Architecture of Country Houses,* published in 1850, the author remarks: "So far as an admiration of foreign style in architecture arises from the mere love of novelty, it is poor and contemptible. ... A villa in the style of a Persian palace (of which there is an example lately erected in Connecticut), with its oriental domes and minarets, equally unmeaning and unsuited to our life or climate, is an example. ..." Downing seems to have heard of a different source of inspiration for Barnum's house from those already mentioned—a Persian palace!

Among the novelties at Iranistan should not be overlooked one that was of a technological nature rather unique for America in the middle of the nineteenth century. Reference is made to a pumping system that supplied a constant flow of water for the fountain that played in the middle of the driveway circle before the front door and for the shower bath adjoining the suite of the owner. Grandeur of effect and personal cleanliness, then, were its objectives. Barnum obtained the unusual by combining exotic styling with the latest in convenience and mechanical contrivances.

25. Gates and stables of Iranistan.
From *The Life of P. T. Barnum.*

26. *"Elephantine Agriculture."*
From P. T. Barnum, *How I Made Millions; or, the Secret of Success,* Chicago and New York, 1884.

We are reminded of another instance in which Barnum blended foreign importation with what purported to be modern utility. The project was presented to the public as "elephantine agriculture." On a six-acre lot bordering the railroad tracks Barnum outfitted an elephant with harness attached to a plow, and equipped his Ceylonese trainer with a timetable. It was their business to be plowing whenever the trains came along. The effect was electrifying! Passengers became excited over the potentialities of elephant farming; and the trains were made to slow down upon passing this revolutionary phenomenon. Letters poured in with all sorts of enquiries on the cost of upkeep and productivity of an elephant. But Barnum's purpose was not agriculture; it was another of his stunts to get publicity for the American Museum. He had leaflets printed discrediting the use of the elephant for farming; and these he mailed out under the heading "strictly confidential." The land was plowed up over sixty times during an interval of two months, after which the animal was sold, and elephant agriculture, for Barum, became a closed matter, though not until an abundance of unfounded information had been circulated, to wit, that elephants could and would do practically all the necessary work around the house and farm, such as washing the windows, feeding the pets and livestock, milking the cows, and taking care of the children, including transporting them to school and putting them to bed.* The elephant, therefore, was supposed to be able to do everything from the chores of the farmhand to those of the nursemaid; and one wonders if by nature he were not better suited to the one round of tasks than the other. In all the publicity Barnum's name kept recurring; and he gloried in the attention it attracted to himself.

* Fred Korotkin, "The Elephant that 'Sold' a Museum," *American Heritage,* Winter 1953–54, p. 50.

Iranistan came near to meeting with disaster in October 1852. It was on the occasion of the marriage of the eldest daughter, when flames and huge volumes of smoke were seen rolling out of the roof of the house. A bucket brigade was quickly formed, and the fire was extinguished without serious damage. But this turned out to be a harbinger of the catastrophe that was to follow five years later. At this time Barnum was stopping at the Astor House in New York. On the morning of 18 December 1857 he received a telegram from his brother, Philo F. Barnum, stating that Iranistan had been reduced to ashes. The alarm had been given at eleven o'clock the previous night, and during the next three hours the building was consumed to the foundations, although most of the furniture and pictures were saved. Insured for only $28,000, Barnum estimated that the loss was in the vicinity of $150,000. The saddened owner then sold the grounds for $50,000 to Elias Howe, Jr. (the inventor of the sewing-machine needle), who intended to erect a new mansion on the estate. But Mr. Howe met an untimely death, and the house never materialized. Was it the incorrigible spirit of Iranistan that refused to be so hastily replaced? A child of mixed parentage, the villa maintains a memorable place in the archives of American architecture for its robust —if unlovely—physiognomy.

LONGWOOD

ALSO INSPIRED by Oriental splendor abroad, as well as designed by an American architect, is Longwood, located several miles below Natchez, Mississippi. Here, however, the Eastern style was seen (by the client) on home soil rather than as interpreted in Western Europe. Dr. Haller Nutt, builder of Longwood, and his family had visited Egypt in order to observe native methods of growing cotton, the crop on which the fortunes of so many Southern planters was based. In addition to obtaining information relating to procedure, Dr. Nutt was anxious to procure seeds of a long-fiber variety of the plant. His mission accomplished on both scores he prepared to return to his estate in Mississippi. Sensing the dangers of international competition, the Egyptian authorities managed to apprehend the package of seeds prior to the departure of the Americans. Afterwards their belongings were thoroughly inspected, and then they were allowed to leave, the Egyptian officials satisfied that their specially developed plant had not left the Black Continent. When Haller Nutt reached home he called his little daughter and asked her to bring him the doll she had carried on their trip. Rip-

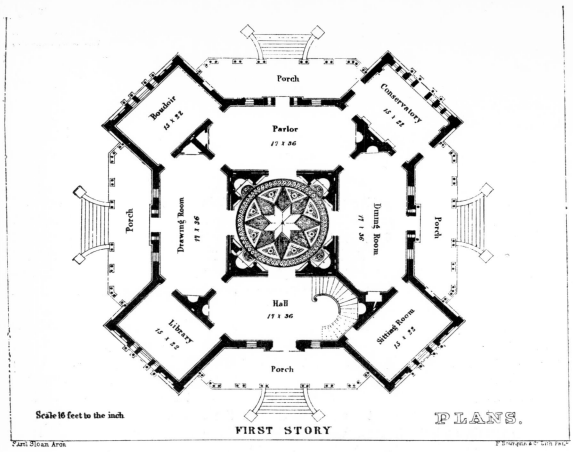

Scale 16 feet to the inch.

PLANS.

FIRST STORY

Saml Sloan Arch't

F Bourquin & C° Lith Pa.t

27. *First story floor plan for a villa in Oriental style.*
From Samuel Sloan, *The Model Architect*, Philadelphia, 1852.

ping a seam he emptied the stuffing, and there, in front of him, lay a heap of the coveted cotton seeds.

In 1852 the Philadelphia architect, Samuel Sloan, published in his two-volume work, *The Model Architect,* a design for a villa in Oriental style. A centrally balanced scheme, the main part of the two-storied house was a regular octagon, the lower floor surrounded by rectangular wing rooms attached to alternate faces, with delicately detailed porches interspersed. The core of the house was an eight-sided rotunda, lighted by a many-faceted belvedere capped by an onion dome. Turret-like spires were affixed to the corners of the forms below to relieve their severity. The floor of the rotunda was to be inlaid in a bold geometric flower motif with pieces of colored glass, affording some light to the basement. The house was appropriate to a site "on the banks of some of our noble streams," said the architect-author, recommending the Hudson or the Mississippi.

Samuel Sloan's recommendation began to materialize at a spot overlooking the Southern river upon his appointment to build Haller Nutt's new home. The published scheme was enlarged. Sloan raised the basement to the status of a full story, one side serving as an entrance at ground level, the balance surrounded by an areaway; and he inserted another floor similar to the main one between it and the octagonal story. Deeply overhanging eaves supported on coupled brackets replaced parapets on the earlier design in *The Model Architect,* which, with the added tier of open galleries,

VERTICAL SECTION

*28. Cross-section of Sloan's Oriental villa design.
From The Model Architect.*

29. Longwood or Nutt's Folly, near Natchez, Mississippi.

was a concession to the tropic location. The dome, too, was enhanced by the setting, "a remembrance of Eastern magnificence which few will judge misplaced as it looms up against the mellow azure of a Southern sky." The architect mentioned also that the peculiar position of the walls—alike in both versions—"mutually strengthen and sustain each other to such a degree as to defy the storms of a torrid clime." The quotations are from another of Sloan's books, *Homestead Architecture*, published at Philadelphia in 1861, featuring Longwood as the initial design, and divulging that it was at that time "being erected by a gentleman in the vicinity of Natchez, Miss."

1861 was the fateful year of the outbreak of the Civil War, which catastrophe overtook building operations at Longwood. The structure had taken form, and there only remained the installation of doors and windows, external stuccoing and internal plastering, and the fitting of fine woodwork and marble facings, when the workmen laid down their tools to enlist in their respective armies. Dr. Nutt prevailed upon a few of them to remain long enough to finish the ground story, where he and his family took up quarters. The villa was never carried any further toward completion; and today one still finds all kinds of tools and building utensils on the upper floors, as though waiting to be taken up and again used in the final work necessary on the house. The marble staircase and sculpture ordered for Longwood were en route from Italy when the war prevented them from reaching their destination. It is rumored that they were put into a Philadelphia mansion. One can speculate upon the gorgeousness of what the decoration would have been had the work at Longwood not been interrupted, a clue to which can be found in the cross-section of *The Model Architect* design, with its lavish detailing of horseshoe arches, mihrab-like alcoves, and dome covering the central rotunda.

The massing of Longwood resembles that of a number of Moslem buildings throughout the East: the Dome of the Rock in Jerusalem, the Tomb of Timur (Tamerlain) at Samarkand, the Mausoleum of Sher Shah Sur at Sasaram, and the Taj Mahal near Agra. The plan, nevertheless, is Western, with partition walls dividing the interior into the rooms proper to an American residence, some of them shaped rather peculiarly due to being divisions of the polygonal overall casing.

Longwood came to be called "Nutt's Folly" on three points: it was never finished, it was of a bizarre Oriental style, and it was an odd shape. Its windows boarded up and the house abandoned, it now stands in mute testimony of a flourishing culture that was obliterated by civil strife. The tropical jungle closes in. The live-oak trees are draped in long streamers of Spanish moss: no festive decorations these, but the tattered and shredded garments worn by a great estate that has seen better days, and fell short of attaining the full measure of its grandeur.

6

BUILT UPON
THE
RIVERS

FLOATING PALACES AND THE INLAND WATERCOURSE

THE ROMANCE and spirit of adventure proper to ships can hardly be equaled in any other sphere of American enterprise. As dependencies the original thirteen colonies had little chance to engage in shipping due to trade monopolies England reserved for herself, but after the signing of the treaty terminating the American Revolution great strides were taken in forwarding the shipping industry. In remarkably short time boats were built in the United States and set out for the most distant ports. Thus was begun a daring and lucrative venture.

Americans proved themselves competent builders of all sorts of craft. Even the limited work of the eighteenth-century shipbuilders of New England showed promise in the manufacture of brigs, or two-masted, square-rigged vessels; and the carvers of figureheads, such as the Skillin brothers of Boston and Samuel McIntire of Salem (and Joseph Wilson of Newburyport, creator of "Lord" Timothy Dexter's gallery of notables), have acquired a modest degree of fame for their work, quite apart from that of the shipwrights. Among America's original contributions to the progress of water transportation may be cited the development of the clipper ship, with slim hull and clouds of billowing sails, a type that got its start in the swift privateers of the War of 1812 and reached maturity during the 1830's. By this time, also, the steam-powered boat was on the way to attaining its full stride. In the 1780's John Fitch of Philadelphia conceived the idea of a boat driven by a steam engine operating twelve paddles. Tried out on the Delaware River it was found to be impractical. Early in the following decade Edward West built a small model of a steamboat in Kentucky, claimed by witnesses to have propelled itself through the water "with great velocity." The crown of success, though, came to rest upon the head of Robert Fulton for the full-scale achievement early in the nineteenth century. First demonstrated on the rivers, it was on the rivers that the steamboat came into its most picturesque flowering.

30. The pilothouse of the "Great Republic."
From Edward King, *The Great South*, Hartford, 1875.

The lure of the American rivers is one of our priceless heritages. Each of the East Coast rivers has its special appeal: the Penobscot and Kennebec rivers in Maine, sites of early fortifications; the Connecticut River that divides Vermont from New Hampshire and traverses Massachusetts to empty into Long Island Sound at Saybrook; the lordly Hudson in New York with its legends of the Catskills; the Delaware and the Susquehanna in Pennsylvania, along which Quakers, Germans, and Scandinavians settled; the little Potomac in Maryland that flows before the portico of Mount Vernon as it skirts Virginia; the Rappahannock and James, the latter famous as a thoroughfare to early Virginia mansions; the Roanoke, Cape Fear, Peedee, and Santee rivers in the Carolinas, and the Savannah and Altamaha in Georgia, each with its stock of fine plantation homes; and Saint Mary's and broad Saint John's River leading to Lake George in Florida. But for sheer size and multiformity of local color all must doff their caps to that great inland watercourse known as the Mississippi. Its banks were settled almost simultaneously by the French, Spanish, and English, and each of these cultures developed together, so that one discovers all sorts of patterns of intermarriage between them, as well as instances of isolation. It was a region of rich soil and abundant water that fostered a host of small agricultural communities of individual personalities. Because of the large productivity of the river country the waterways loomed in importance. The new civilization could be seen growing from day to

*31. A race by moonlight: the "Queen of the
West" sends up a rocket as she out-
strips the "Morning Star."*
Currier and Ives print, 1866.

day, and although of mixed parentage, in intent it was very much American—schooled
and tempered by the mighty Mississippi.

The Mississippi takes its name from the Algonquin language, meaning "great river,"
sometimes interpreted as "father river" or "gathering in of all the waters." It is not
a single stream, of course, but a family of watercourses embracing about forty tributaries, of which the Missouri River is the longest (nearly three thousand miles). The
entire system drains over a million square miles of land, or upwards of one-third the

area of the United States. Arising in the marshes and lakes of northern Minnesota the Mississippi proper is quite shallow as far as Minneapolis, after which the river becomes deeper and in places very wide, from here down to Cape Girardeau, Missouri, thirty miles beyond which it joins the Ohio, "La Belle Rivière," at Cairo. Although only six hundred miles straight south from here to the Gulf, bends in the channel make the gauging by water seventeen hundred miles. In the lower stretch the hills keep their distance, which often has given the river opportunity to overflow its course, flooding its muddy waters over the lowlands, prompting the expenditure of much money on the building of levees in defense of it. After rounding the crescent at New Orleans the river meets the delta—an obstacle it has deposited in its own path—and through five chief openings the Mississippi is at last united with the sea. In all that great organism called the Mississippi there are over fifteen thousand miles of navigable waterways. And not only did the river traffic become one of the leading businesses in this country, it became one of the most colorful.

The steamboat that plowed the rivers is a fitting symbol of mid- to late-nineteenth-century America and Americans. Here were combined the spirit of adventure and of exploration, the love of travel, trade and transportation, the embodiment of mechanical ingenuity and skill in manipulation, the realization of power and speed, and the display of wealth and attainment of luxury idealized by our forebears. Surely we can share their enthusiasm for the broad, handsome boats with massive, spinning paddle-wheels and great black plumes floating overhead. There was something fascinating about those bulging forms that seemed to hover over the water like a magic carpet, their plush and gilded interiors aglow like Aladdin's palace. Desirable subjects they were in the popular art of their times, issued by numerous printmakers, among whom Messrs. Currier and Ives were foremost in variety, appeal, execution, and sales. Notable favorites were the scenes of boat races.

When it was decided that two boats were to compete the news was announced weeks in advance, and at the appointed time people would line the shores all along the course chosen for the race. Although most of the spectators did not hear of the outcome until long afterwards, they would get a thrill out of seeing what lap they could. Mark Twain related that prior to the staging of a race "the whole Mississippi Valley was in a state of consuming excitement. Politics and the weather were dropped, and people talked only of the coming race. As the time approached, the two steamers 'stripped' and got ready. Every encumbrance that added weight, or exposed a resisting surface to wind or water, was removed, if the boat could possibly do without it. The 'spars', and sometimes even their supporting derricks, were sent ashore, and no means left to set the boat afloat in the case she got aground." Every effort was made on the part of the captain and crew to acquire the coveted gilded buckhorns awarded to the fleetest boat. Among the outstanding contests were those between the "Eclipse" and the "Natchez" before the Civil War, between the "Queen of the West" and "Morning Star" in 1866, and between the "Natchez" and the "Robert E. Lee" in 1870. Extremely dramatic were the prints of the races shown at night with the moon etching the tattered clouds and scattering its beams on the river, the dark shapes along the banks silhouetted against

32. Saloon of the "Grand Republic."
After an old photograph.

the water, the patches of light on the boats and the streamers of luminous smoke, and the clean white curve of a rocket set off as a braggard's salute from the deck of the winning ship.

The first steamboat on the Western waters, christened the "New Orleans," was built by Nicholas Roosevelt from plans by Robert Fulton and launched at Pittsburgh in 1811. During the 1820's the steamer had become a familiar sight on the Mississippi, and by the 1840's "steamboatin'" was an established institution. In addition to Pittsburgh steam packets were manufactured at Cincinnati, Jeffersonville, New Albany, and Saint Louis. At this time the hull had all but disappeared beneath the waterline. On a flat oval tray stood a two-storied structure entirely surrounded by galleries, except where the gigantic cylinder covering over the sidewheels cut through the brim of the boat. The lower deck was for cargo and the stacks of fuel to feed the ravenous engines that belched forth heavy jet fumes when seasoned with a little pitch. A double, usually curving, staircase ascended to the main deck above. Down the center of the boat stretched the public room or "saloon," lighted by a clerestory raised above the level of the rows of private cabins that looked out on the decks. The pilothouse was over the saloon, up front, a little behind the twin smokestacks that sometimes reached a height of eighty feet. Somewhat later—about mid century—a "Texas" (the latest annex), or third story serving as crew's quarters, elevated the pilothouse still higher.

The ornateness of the better boats won for them the designation of "floating palaces." Motifs for elaboration of each pier, arch, and frame were borrowed from every conceivable source. Undoubtedly the boat with the most gorgeous cabin was the "Grand Republic," a rebuilding and enlargement of the "Great Republic" (originally con-

structed in 1867), which occurred in 1876. In its later dress the saloon took on the aspect of a make-believe cathedral with nave and side aisles separated by two parallel rows of colonnettes supporting frilly-edged ribs with spandrels filled with spider-web lacework. The ceiling areas of the "nave" were decorated with wheel designs aping French rose windows. The three-part division on axis, however, was not common to

33. *Remodeled drawing room of the Le Vert house, Mobile, Alabama.*
Restored furnishings conjectural.

river-boat saloons; indeed, in this one example it was perhaps unique. Yet the lavishness of the "Grand Republic" was typical of saloons in general.

Similar décor was applied to interiors of homes, particularly in the South where people had a flair for this sort of thing. In an old house in Mobile, Alabama, once owned by Madame Octavia Walton Le Vert, known at home and abroad as the "Belle of the Union," the daughter of Andrew Jackson's Secretary of State and author of several works describing her journeys, including *Souvenirs of Travel* (1857), a renovation resulted in a spectacle of steamboat magnificence, though not until sometime after Mme. Le Vert had terminated her regime in the house. The delicate modeling of fluid rococo marble mantels contrasted abruptly with a high dado of rectangular panels; and the heavy sweep of a thick, low arch springing from squat pillars was equally at odds with an open screen on slender posts, with elongated dolphin bodies incorporated in a trelliswork of lozenges, concentric circles, and stylized rinceau, the airiness of which would have done justice to the finest of floating palaces, as may be seen through a comparison of it with the saloon of the "Grand Republic." It is "floating palace" design at its most striking and characteristic best.

STEAMBOAT GOTHIC

MANY OF the world's great civilizations have been linked to a river. In Egypt the green, fertile valley of the Nile contrasted sharply with the desert wastelands that lay beyond. Life depended upon the autumnal inundation of the stream, which meant the start of a new year, a new cycle of growth. The Egyptian's thoughts were so much centered upon the river that he oriented himself toward the cryptic source of the Nile and used a single word to mean "face" (*i.e.* "facing toward") and "south"; and all Egyptians understood what he meant. To the eastward a series of remarkable cultures succeeded one another in Mesopotamia, the "Land between the Rivers," the Tigris and Euphrates. In India the earliest civilizations centered on the Indus River and then shifted to the Ganges, the river sacred to the Hindus, named after the goddess Gangā, eldest daughter of Himavat. In China the Yellow River was the center of fabled ancient dynasties and then shared with the Yangtze the seat of early empires. In Europe, likewise, great nations flourished along the rivers—the Volga, Danube, Rhine, and Seine. Indeed the important European capitals are located on rivers rather than sea or ocean. Although the American population first clung to the Eastern seacoast so long as its ties were fastened to the Old World, once independent a whole new and variegated culture came into being—as has been noted—in remarkably short time along the inland river system.

Technological advances achieved by man in the nineteenth century played an important role in determining the trend taken by civilization along the Mississippi. This

34. House at Mundy's Landing on the Kentucky River.

was something that had never happened—in fact something that had never had the opportunity to happen—before. Existence was geared largely to transportation facilities invested in steamboats, and this was reflected nowhere better than in house design, where not only interiors but the overall exterior shape of the house as well was affected by steamers. The vogue began with the utilitarian adjunct of open galleries, such as those added to a residence at Mundy's Landing on the Kentucky River probably during the 1840's. The square piers and flat entablatures were concessions to the then-popular Greek Revival mode of dryland architecture, their bulkiness not at all boat-like. The next step toward a more nautical effect, taken during the 1850's, was to slenderize the posts, make the cornices thinner, and forms bowed. These appear at "Hill Forest," the home of Thomas Goff at the head of Main Street overlooking the Ohio River and the town of Aurora, Indiana. The style of Hill Forest is Italianate, displaying arched openings, coupled windows, quoins at the corners, brackets under the eaves, and Tuscan columns; but the round pilothouse, flat roofs, curving decks, and light wood construction all bespeak the indebtedness of the house to the steamboat.

Although the two houses referred to lack the ornateness usually associated with floating palaces of the last century, a host of other examples may be enumerated on which gingerbread was applied without inhibition. Longwood, the Oriental house at Natchez, is one. But we need not turn to such an imposing edifice. A small house at 2002 Washington Street in Vicksburg, Mississippi, has accumulated a lion's share of ornamentation, especially in the upper part, around the gable, widow's walk, and belvedere. Evidently of *fin de siècle* vintage one denotes a suggestion of Eastlake influence. In terms of style, the houses under discussion can be categorized as Steamboat Greek Revival, Steamboat Italianate, Steamboat Saracenic (Longwood), and Steamboat East-

lakian.* The best known classification is Steamboat Gothic, which we have already seen illustrated in the saloon of the steamer "Grand Republic." The Steamboat Gothic style had a tremendous appeal for Americans and often was used on residences having no functional feature peculiar to boats.

The name "Steamboat Gothic" so fascinated the novelist Mrs. Frances Parkinson Keyes that she chose it for the title to a book and then set to work to write a story

* The author's "Floating Palaces Aground," *Art News*, September 1950, p. 29.

35. Hill Forest, Aurora, Indiana.

to go with it. For setting she adopted an old house thirty miles upstream from New Orleans near Reserve, Louisiana, known as "San Francisco" ("Cindy Lou" in the story), which the hero of the fiction—a former gambler—purchases in the opening pages. Mrs. Keyes' descriptions are fairly faithful to the house itself, other than once mentioning the bedrooms as being on an upper floor (above the main floor), which they are not.

The Louisiana plantation house was built about 1849 by a Frenchman, M. Valsin

36. Superstructure of a house at Vicksburg, Mississippi.

Marmillion. The cost is said to have exceeded Mr. Marmillion's means, leaving him penniless, which condition he memorialized in christening the place "Sans Fruscin" (without a cent). Later, through misunderstanding, the name became transposed into that of the kindly medieval saint of Assisi. The house was typical of lower-Mississippi domestic architecture in having a high basement story, which raised the main floor a good eight feet above ground level. In addition to the kitchen and wine room, an office and a couple of bedrooms are on the lower floor, whereas the principal bedrooms are to the rear of the twin parlors above, placed around the long dining hall at the back of the house. Exclusively French, two of the six chambers are without outside exposures, opening only into the central hall and adjacent rooms. If by this means they remain cooler during the hot summer months, by the same token they relinquish their rights to direct daylight and fresh air.

Now concealed from the river by the high levee that borders this stretch of the

37. *Ceiling detail of southwest chamber of "San Francisco" plantation, Reserve, Louisiana.*

Mississippi, one comes upon San Francisco around a bend in the road. The spectacle, beheld so suddenly, seems unbelievable—like an apparition out of some weird and wonderful dream. A double staircase of two flights leads up to the verandah encircled by Corinthian columns supporting Tudor arches, with a deep overhanging balcony and a bracketed and shuttered gallery above. The low-pitched hipped roof is pierced by dormers that have diamond-paned windows at front and sides; and there is a clerestory pent, with a railing around its summit different from that of the balcony, verandah, or staircase, no two of which are alike. The house may look somewhat top-heavy, which only contributes to its illusion of unreality. Within the verandah that extends across the front and half-way down each flank are the twin parlors and a central hall that is entered through a wide doorway, over which a long lozenge and pair of stars carved in the frieze serve as keynote insignia of the house. Two circular water towers of cypress wood elevated on brick cylinders are to right and left of the plantation domicile that epitomizes the Steamboat Gothic style.

The hall and parlors are separated by screens of columns matching those of the verandah, and by tremendous doors. The interior colors are light and cheerful: off-white woodwork, yellow walls, and pale-grayish-lavender frieze and ceiling, the upper part of the room decorated with painted flowers, trellis work, and birds. These are organized into a large central wheel on the ceiling, somewhat Adamesque in design, offset by corner motifs and borders, creating the sensation of a garden. In the southwest bedroom the pinkish-gray ceiling is covered with trellises, except for an oval of sky blue in the middle where several dark-skinned winged cherubs frolic with sprays of posies. Dominique Canova (a nephew of the famous Italian sculptor, Antonio), whose brush painted the dome of the Saint Louis Hotel and vaults of the Saint Louis Cathedral in New Orleans, executed the decorations at San Francisco. The ceiling paintings are on wood rather than plaster, possibly to assure their remaining in place.

The dining room centered at the rear of the house is remarkable for its long and narrow shape—sixteen by thirty-six feet—with a stairway at each end leading down to the kitchen. A sizeable gathering of diners could be seated at a single extended table. Narrow stairways in the two chambers at the back corners of the building ascend to what was to have been the crowning achievement of San Francisco, the great ball-room, over sixty by seventy feet in extent, completely surrounded by a balcony, lighted by the diamond-paned dormers and through the jade and amber, azure and lavender colored glass of the topmost clerestory, which, even on the silvered timbers of the unfinished attic, create an atmosphere of mystic loveliness. How enchanting would have been the vision of this hall in its completed state, undoubtedly also embellished

38. *General view of "San Francisco" plantation.*

by Dominique Canova's facile brushwork! One is challenged to visualize what the effect would have been: the cavern-like room, the rainbow hues dancing in geometric patterns about the polished floor and skipping in shattered shapes over the sloping wall surfaces, breezes perfumed by honeysuckle and wistaria drifting in through the louvred shutters, a glimpse out over the broad green lawn down to the quiet river, where a packet flourishing twin plumes of black rides into view and gives a whistle salute to San Francisco, a fully arrayed knight-errant of the mighty Mississippi passing in review, rendering homage to the bejeweled queen, splendidly enthroned!

GEO-FORMS

BARREL HOUSES

BY THIS time it must be apparent to the reader that there have been many Americans whose ideas about home construction have gone around in circles; and so now we come without surprise to a group whose constructed homes go around them in circles. Reference is made to the practice of residing in round houses.

The circular structure in America boasts a venerable history. The aboriginal peoples of North America made use of round shelters: half-spherical and conic tepees of thatch, bark, or animal skins stretched over a light framework of saplings in the Eastern woodlands; great, earth-packed domical family houses in the Midwest; elevated, cylindrical granaries along the lower Mississippi River; and underground circular *kivas* in the Southwest. The early European colonists also put up round buildings. The "Old Stone Mill" in Newport, Rhode Island, used by Governor Benedict Arnold for a windmill about 1700, a round tower supported on eight crude arches springing from an equal number of stone piers, is thought either to have been erected by the Norsemen as a fortified church during the twelfth or the thirteenth century, or built by Governor Arnold himself at the end of the seventeenth century, originally to serve as an observatory and later converted into a mill when the town's need for one arose.* In Virginia, the south extremities of the two wings of the colonial capitol (1705) at Williamsburg were semicircular; a round dovecote exists at Shirley, a pre-Revolution plantation in Charles City County; and early ice houses throughout the state generally were of this shape, such as that incorporated into the north service wing of Jefferson's Monticello. Thomas Jefferson made a sketch in 1794 for a circular retreat having a round central saloon and two elliptical rooms with a colonnade encircling the perimeter. Jefferson's later design for the University of Virginia featured parallel rows of

* W. S. Godfrey, Jr., "The Newport Puzzle," *Archaeology*, Autumn 1949, pp. 146–49; "Newport Tower II," *ibid.*, Summer 1950, pp. 82–86.

39. The Southwick house, Middletown, Rhode Island.

buildings facing a wide lawn that was terminated at the south end by a rotunda library modeled on the Pantheon at Rome.* Benjamin Latrobe proposed a round house for Robert Liston, British Minister to the United States.† The English architect John Plaw had published a circular residence plan in his *Rural Architecture*, printed at London

---

* I. T. Frary, *Thomas Jefferson: Architect and Builder*, Richmond, 1939, Pl. XLIII. The drawings referred to may be found reproduced in Fiske Kimball, *Thomas Jefferson, Architect*, Boston and Cambridge, 1916.

† Fiske Kimball, *Domestic Architecture of the American Colonies and of the Early Republic*, New York, 1927, Fig. 135 (p. 175).

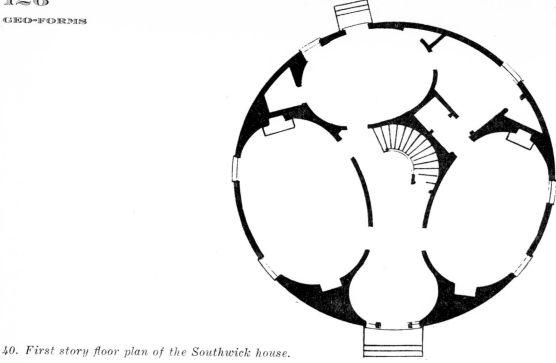

40. First story floor plan of the Southwick house.

in 1744 (Plates XXV–XXX), which may have suggested their schemes to Jefferson and Latrobe. The Federal period witnessed the construction of numerous residences with projecting rooms of curved shape. William Thornton's Octagon in Washington, of 1798, contains a circular entrance hall, a small version of the rotunda in the national capitol by the same architect. The Swan House in Dorchester, Massachusetts, has a round drawing room protruding at the front, a tall tubiform that dominates lower forms to either side, somewhat resembling the massing of the steamboat house at Aurora, Indiana.*

The practical domestic cylinder in America belongs primarily to the last three quarters of the nineteenth century, patronized as much, or more, by obscure builders as by well known architects.

The double-family house of Seth Strong, a brick mason of Northampton, Massachusetts, was built in 1827, a two-storied tub shape having a conic roof, housing two parlors, two living rooms, and two dining rooms in sets on either side of a central hall on the first floor. The rooms are separated by right-angled partitions as though belonging to a rectangular plan. The reasons given for the overall shape—according to the testimony of Mr. Strong's daughter in an interview early in this century—are that, first, it would stand up well against wind and storm (presage to Longwood?), and, second, it would hold heat better than any other form.† An ell at the rear supplementing the big cylinder has led to the place becoming nicknamed the "Jew's-Harp House."

Within the next dozen years the concept of rotund houses had crystallized into some-

* *Ibid.*, Figs. 122–23 (pp. 162–63).

† Walter L. Creese, "Round Houses in New England," *Old-Time New England*, April-June 1953, p. 85.

thing quite definite. In Middletown, Rhode Island, an example was constructed about 1841, either by Joseph or Christopher Southwick, the property passing from one to the other on August 3rd of that year. Both Southwicks were shipwrights. The house was built of wood, the siding planks applied horizontally, bent into a gentle curve like the facing of a boat hull. The circular roof was concave and crowned by a glazed belvedere similar in form to the house proper. The outstanding attraction of the residence is its plan: the main hall flares wide at either end to create an entrance vestibule at the outer wall and a space for the circular staircase at the center of the house; around this hall are disposed oval-and odd-shaped rooms. The arrangement somewhat resembles that of the truncated column of M. de Monville near Paris, only the interior volume of the Rhode Island house is not chopped into so many tiny anterooms, and exhibits an easy flow from one space into the next. Of interest in this connection is a persisting tradition that the idea of building a circular house came to Southwick at a dance being held in a square house, upon which occasion he noted that the couples could not swing freely enough to the music. One wonders whether he entertained extensively with dancing parties in his own new house in order to justify its circularity.

Another annular house of wood in New England is at Somerville, Massachusetts. It was built for Enoch Robinson, apparently during the mid 1850's. The reason for the roundness here was uniqueness. Robinson, a few years earlier, had built a house in the Italian-villa style, only to see it copied by an admiring neighbor, and became so enraged that he vowed to build a house that nobody could duplicate. However, in plan, the circular Robinson house shows about the same relationship of parlor to stairhall that one finds in the earlier Southwick house, though the front lobby is separated from the stairhall, the first room on the right (the library) is perfectly round, and the other two rooms (dining room and kitchen) are wedge shaped. The window spacing is more uniform than in the Middletown house, regimented between vertical battens on the outside. Here our thoughts return to the de Monville column with fenestration determined by perpendicular flutings, exactly twice the number of the Robinson bays. That the French *folie* may have served as model for the Massachusetts house is suggested by the fact that the American builder collected continental tomes, and perhaps possessed the published drawings of the Désert de Retz in Le Rouge's *Jardins Anglo-Chinois.** The plans of the Enoch Robinson house in turn were reproduced in a book entitled, *The House: A Pocket Manual of Rural Architecture,* by Daniel Harrison Jacques, gotten out in 1859 by Fowler and Wells of New York. We shall hear more later about Orson Squire Fowler, one of the partners in the publishing firm.

* *Ibid.,* pp. 87–88.

Coincidental with the appearance of the plan of the Robinson dwelling in *The House* another round dwelling was constructed at Plympton, Massachusetts, by one Zenus M. Washburn, a spiritualist, who gave as an excuse for the selection of this shape the inability of evil spirits to hide in a round house. The rooms, however, were right-angled, like those in the Seth Strong house. The two-story building was covered with horizontal weatherboarding.

Late-nineteenth-century residential cylinders designed by name architects include the Daniel S. Newhall house at Jamestown, Rhode Island, conceived by the builder's architect friend, none other than Charles Follen McKim, in the mid 1880's. Perched on a promontory, the porch is atop a huge rock that penetrates the lower story of the house, where service quarters are located. The living room, off the porch, occupies the center of the main upper level, and from it open the various pie-shaped chambers.* The outer walls are surfaced with shingles. The Newhall house is across the sound from Newport, with Middletown and the Southwick house only a few miles away. Another *fin-de-siècle* example got no further than on paper. The octogenarian architect, Alexander Jackson Davis, owned a place called "Wildmont" on Orange Mountain in New Jersey. Originally built in 1856 around a spiral staircase taken from a tower of the William Waddell villa at Fifth Avenue and Thirty-seventh Street in New York City, the house at Wildmont had been rebuilt following a fire in 1884. Sketched on the last page of the architect's professional diary in the Metropolitan Museum of Art are plans of 1891 for reconstructing the house anew on a wheel design. Unfortunately, Davis died the following year, and nothing came of it.

The fascination of conceiving cylindrical houses continued into the twentieth century. A design for one by William Greenwood was reproduced in the issue of *House Beautiful* for June 1908 (pp. 41–42). W. K. Boyne constructed a three-storied barrel house at Centerville, on Cape Cod, in the late 1930's. One of the most recent round houses worthy of recognition is that called "Toy Hill," built at Pleasantville, New York, after a design by Frank Lloyd Wright, the house composed of two interpenetrating circles of varying radii, connected by a long wall along the ridge of a rise to a circular carport, a disk supported umbrella-fashion on a single pier.† The same architect's round scheme for the Guggenheim Museum in New York, with its helical exhibition gallery, may end all circular building projects, or else be the cause of a new resurgence of them. Finally, domestic circularity received momentous acclaim in 1946 when

---

* The author's "Transportation Design Elements in American Architecture," *American Quarterly*, Fall 1956, Fig. 7 (p. 207).

† *Architectural Forum: the Magazine of Building*, January 1951, pp. 98–/101/.

Beech Aircraft began manufacturing aluminum and plexiglass houses of pumpkin shape designed by Richard Buckminster Fuller, originator of the "dymaxion house" of 1927, a hexagonal affair skewered on a central mast a story above ground level. The later Fuller house comes ready made, requiring only to be assembled upon arrival at the site and set upon low foundations prepared for it; and, being mass-produced, it shows that the barrel house has aroused and met the needs of modern American demands.

CORNERS PLENTIFUL

CORNERLESS round houses bear a striking resemblance to houses having more corners than the usual four, in compactness of form and plan and in the fitting together of odd-shaped rooms for interesting interior effects. There seems nothing strange about this if one stops to consider that the greater the number of angles to a regular polygon the correspondingly greater the number of sides, and hence the nearer its approach to the circle—the infinitude of flat sides becoming unified into a single continuous curve. Prismatic buildings are more prevalent throughout the United States than cylindrical structures.

The polygon came to America with European colonists to serve all kinds of purposes. In Pennsylvania, New Jersey, and New York it determined the shape of seventeenth-century Dutch churches, such as the Reformed Church at Rensselaerswyck, for which Kiliaen Van Rensselaer in 1641 furnished a wooden model accompanied by a letter calling attention to the fact that its construction was like that of a windmill.* Similar churches were to be found at Bergen, Jamaica, New Utrecht, Hackensack, Flatbush, and Brooklyn, all now demolished. The octagonal shape long had been employed in Christian architecture, traceable back to Byzantine churches and Romanesque baptisteries, the number of sides symbolizing the eighth day of the new era added to the old Jewish seven-day week. Application in early American churches favored acoustics and seating arrangement, whereby the pews were divided into three blocks separated by aisles, those of the inner block at right angles to the central axis of the church, and the outer running parallel to the diagonal walls, so that all more nearly faced the pulpit. The English also employed octagons and other polygons for churches. At Richmond,

* Turpin C. Bannister, "The Architecture of the Octagon in New York State," *New York History,* January 1945, pp. 45–46.

Vermont, stands the sixteen-sided Union Church, dating from 1812, built by the carpenter William Rhodes. The church is of substantial size in order to accommodate the amalgamated congregations of five Protestant sects.*

Early forts incorporated polygons for better observation facilities and defense, as in the shingled, eight-sided blockhouse (1812) at Edgecombe, Maine, having an overhanging second story and a tall, slender lookout atop the low pyramid roof. Fort McClary, built at Kittery Point the same year of stone with wood overhang, was pentagonal.† At Wiscasset, also in Maine, a powder house is of circular shape; and familiar to everyone is the octagonal powder magazine (1714) at colonial Williamsburg, down in Virginia.

The octagon was as much favored for school houses during the early nineteenth century as it had been for churches upwards of a hundred years earlier. The primary reason for the popularity of the shape has to do with the absolute authority of the single schoolmaster, whose desk was placed on the side facing the door, where he could watch everyone entering or leaving; the benches and desks of the male students encircled the three walls to the teacher's right, and those of the girls the three to his left. When the master made his inspection rounds he could return to his desk without retracing his steps. In the center of the room stood the stove, in winter radiating heat evenly to all sides. Most of these buildings were built of stone; one, near the village of Oxford Valley, Falls Township, Pennsylvania, displays a date stone that reads 1775, but it is generally assumed that the present building was constructed over half a century later. Often referred to as the "eight square" school houses, other Pennsylvania examples are to be found at Montandon in Northumberland County and on the Bath Road in Nazareth Township. Though multiple-sided school houses seem most at home in Pennsylvania, the distribution exceeds the limits of the state. Examples are located in the vicinity of Darlington, Maryland (this one hexagonal), at Leipsic, Delaware, and at Fairview New Jersey.‡

Dependencies and farm buildings on large Southern estates were ofttimes polygonal. Along the Mississippi River, *pigeonniers* or dovecotes at Uncle Sam Plantation, that once stood near Convent, Louisiana, were six sided. At Parlange, on False River (near New Roads), they are eight sided. *Garçonnières* at Houmas (Convent vicinity) and Melrose (above Baton Rouge) also are octagonal. Early-nineteenth-century accessory

* Walter Creese, "Fowler and the Domestic Octagon," *Art Bulletin*, June 1946, p. 90 Fig. 1 (facing p. 98).

† Hugh Morrison, *Early American Architecture*, New York, 1952, p. 76.

‡ Photographs of the last three may be found in the collection of the Historic American Buildings Survey, Library of Congress.

41. Poplar Forest, Jefferson's octagonal retreat near Lynchburg, Virginia.
Restored to appearance before the fire of 1845, based on elevation drawing by
Cornelia J. Randolph, *ca.* 1820.

buildings to the houses at 91 Beaufain Street, 14 Legare Street, and 138 Wentworth
Street in Charleston, South Carolina, are many sided; the last is a bath house.* An
octagonal garden house is at Montpelier in Virginia. Upper Brandon has several polygonal out buildings.† George Washington's Mount Vernon is enhanced by an octagonal garden house, which significantly was used as a school room. Washington constructed a brick and frame sixteen-sided barn at Dogue Run Farm in 1793.‡ It proved
quite practical for cows having a wider frame aft than fore, thereby fitting neatly
into the wedge-shaped stalls encompassing the innermost fodder trough. Barns of this
type are scattered throughout the Eastern, Central, and Midwestern states.

Thomas Jefferson designed a couple of garden temples early in the 1770's, presumably to ornament the grounds at Monticello, these having respectively, two or four
rooms flanking an octagon. The cruciform plan of the original residence on Jefferson's
little mountain had three arms ending in octagonal bays—the fourth being the portico

* The first and third are illustrated in the Carolina Art Association, *This Is Charleston*, Charles-
ton, 1944, pp. 9, 111.
† A good many polygonal garden houses and dependencies are shown throughout Alice G. B.
Lockwood, *Gardens of Colony and State*, New York, 1934, 2 vols.
‡ Creese, *op. cit.*, Fig. 4 (facing p. 98).

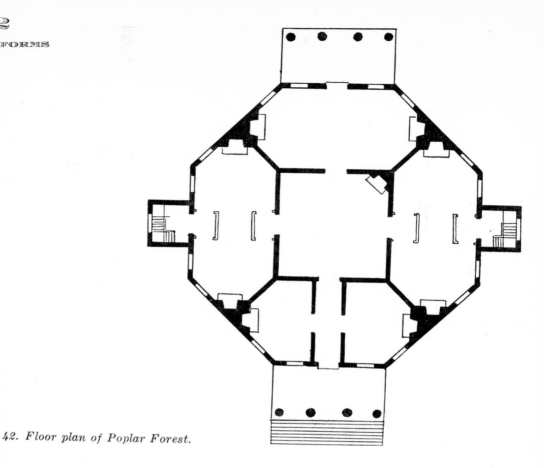

42. *Floor plan of Poplar Forest.*

—and when the depth of the house was doubled, beginning in the 1790's, two more octagons were added. Jefferson once wrote to a prospective guest at the time Monticello was undergoing changes: "We shall have the eye of a brick kiln to poke you in or an octagon to air you in." One of his designs proposes an eight-sided pavilion set on the terrace at each corner of the depressed service wings, but it was not actualized. In all, over fifty plans for buildings by Jefferson manifest some octagonal architectural feature.*

The most distinctive of Jefferson's octagonal reveries took the form of a retreat to which he escaped from the hordes of guests that sometimes overran Monticello. It was built at Poplar Forest, a farm he owned near Lynchburg, some sixty or seventy miles southwest of Charlottesville. The plan had been conceived for a house at Pantops for his daughter, Maria, and son-in-law, John W. Eppes, which project came to a sad standstill with the death of Maria in 1804. The house at Poplar Forest was intended to be used occasionally by Jefferson during his lifetime, after which it was to pass to his grandson, Francis Eppes, together with a sizeable piece of the 4,627 acres of land over which the house presided.

The octagon retreat at Poplar Forest had brick walls and a low hipped roof, pedimented porticoes expanded at front and rear, and two tiny stair turrets were affixed to

* Facsimiles of Jefferson's drawings were published by Fiske Kimball, *Thomas Jefferson, Architect*, Boston and Cambridge, 1916.

opposite faces on a cross axis. The form had a fifty-three-foot diameter, or twenty-two feet to a side. Although a single-storied building, a sunken hemicycle extending from the back of one of the stair appendages to the other brought the lower level above ground. There was no railing to the platform of the porch thus elevated, yet an elaborate balustrade superimposed upon the cornice graced the flanks of the building and continued out to the corners of the porticoes. A square room in the center of the house was the dining hall, around the perimeter of which were elongated octagonal interiors, the front one portioned into two small chambers by a passageway. The adjoining rooms could be divided into two each by a system of screens, circulation to the stairways afforded through whichever section happened to be unoccupied. The remaining apartment was the drawing room opening onto the rear portico. Four chimneys were connected to fireplaces in the ends of the oblong rooms, with windows close by giving pleasant vistas of the countryside. An additional fireplace was in one corner of the dining hall, which, the largest room and centrally located, was meant to be the family gathering place, as in so many Southern homes. The dining hall probably had a high ceiling and was lighted through a skylight. Poplar Forest burned about twenty years after Jefferson's decease, and in rebuilding it was simplified and altered. Even so, with balustrades omitted, the roof planes rising to a common apex, and several windows walled up, enough exists of the original scheme to convey something of the rare ingenuity of the designer in utilizing the polygonal shape in this his *folie*.

The influence of Thomas Jefferson, being a spirited public figure, was to be expected no less in eight-cornered architecture than in other fields. A direct and personal transfer took place in the work of the young architect Robert Mills, who had received some of his early training from Jefferson and had made drawings of some of his teacher's buildings. Mill's own octagonal designs include the Octagon Unitarian Church (1813) at Philadelphia, and the Monumental Church (after 1811) in Richmond, Virginia, for which city the architect also designed an eight-sided city hall. John Haviland's Eastern State Penitentiary (1823–35) in Philadelphia had cell wings radiating from an octagon in order to expedite the passage of prisoners to and from the assemblies in the central block; and castellated eight-sided towers projected from the corners of the great stone outer walls. A house having no right-angled corners and no parallel walls was erected at Petersburg, Virginia, in 1815; its peculiar physiognomy—like the round Washburn house at Plympton, Massachusetts—was supposed to ward off evil spirits. Called "Trapezium Place," the builder was an eccentric Irishman, by the name of Charles O'Hara, who acted on the advice of a West Indian servant. The house is often referred to as "Rat Castle." The octagon proved of practical value for the display of objects. The Woods building, or "Nineveh Gallery," at Amherst College was constructed after 1846 to house the geological and archeological collections. Floral Hall of the Maxwell Springs Fair Association (of which society Jefferson had been made an honorary member about 1816) was built at Lexington, Kentucky, in 1880, and it also was octagonal, the plants exhibited on concentric tiers around the perimeter of the hall, where they were readily visible to the visitors from anywhere in the center.* An extension of the list would not prove anything further, and so we turn without more ado to the role of the octagon in Yankee residences.

FOWLER'S FOLLY AND THE HOME FOR ALL

THE BUILDING of octagonal domiciles was one of the top architectural fads in America from the middle of the nineteenth century onward. The craze may be traced to a single individual, a philosopher of sorts, a lecturer, a writer, and publisher on a wide range of subjects, by name, Orson Squire Fowler, a gentleman who himself built and occupied an eight-sided house at Fishkill, New York, and thus spoke from personal experience and with authority on the subject.

The use of octagons in earlier permanent dwellings, like the use of other structural octagons—as stated previously—seems clearly to have come to America from Europe. William Kent reproduced octafaceted plans for baronial houses in his *Designs of Inigo Jones* (published in London, 1727, Vol. II, Plates 17 and 18), a copy of which was in the library of Thomas Jefferson and in all likelihood inspired his occasional abode at Poplar Forest, though considerably reduced in size and simplified in room arrangement sympathetic to its intention. The best known American polygon of the Federal era is the late-eighteenth-century house at the intersection of New York Avenue and Eighteenth Street in Washington, mentioned some pages back in connection with its projecting round entrance motif. The name of this house, "The Octagon," built for Col. John Tayloe, is a misnomer, by reason of its having six rather than eight flat sides. However, four of its half-dozen corners are those of a regular octagon; the remaining pair are right angles, following the shape of the principal rooms embraced by them. With two sides of the house parallel to the streets, the layout is admirably suited to the corner lot on which the building is situated. The Octagon seems to have begotten several offsprings, one on the outskirts of New Hope, Pennsylvania—"Cintra" or

* The author's *Back Streets and Pine Trees*, Lexington, 1956, pp. 88–89.

43. Fowler's Folly, Fishkill, New York.

"Maris' Folly" (*ca.* 1816, described at the conclusion of the section on "The Marble Palace")—and the other at a street corner in Portsmouth, New Hampshire, the three-storied Admiral Storer house, unfortunately demolished in 1880.*

Though occasional examples of polygonal houses appeared before and during the early 1800's, the adoption of the eight-sided prism to home construction on a wide scale was due largely to creative thinking on the part of Orson Squire Fowler, and may have served as residence for this remarkable man had no building of similar figure previously existed in this country. Fowler possessed an independent sense of values, eschewing generally accepted fashions and opinions, as shown by his condemnation of ladies wearing tight corsets and other binding garments and his insistence upon the ill effects of taking stimulants (including tea, coffee, and tobacco along with alcohol) and of the carnivorous diet. His consuming interest was phrenology, in which field he converted and trained many practitioners in the art of interpreting cranium bumps and bulges. The enthusiasm over phrenology did not long survive him, but Fowler's lasting contribution to the American scene was made in the building line.

Fowler published a book in 1848, entitled *A Home for All; or, The Gravel Wall and Octagon Mode of Building,* and simultaneously began construction of his eight-sided house at Fishkill. The house, of course, was given a prominent place among the plates in the book. It was a large dwelling of four full stories and a cupola, the two lower floors circumscribed by porches and the upper stories by balconies. The building was relatively free of ornamentation or stylistic references, its elements having a forthright quality suggestive of contemporary architecture, which is noteworthy in view of the fact that the majority of houses of the period were romantically beholding to historic styles for their primary appeal. Fowler's, by contrast, was refreshingly functional and void of sentimental overtones.

The chief characteristic of the house—its eight-sidedness—was defended by the author on economic, practical, and aesthetic grounds. The octagon provided more usable volume than an ordinary rectangular building, the author noted: "the nearer spherical our houses, the more inside room for the outside wall...the octagon, by approximating to the circle, incloses more space for its wall than the square." Besides obtaining maximum living space for constructed surfaces, there was the factor of heat loss being less in compact masses than in lengthy structures. The expense of extra angles thus was compensated for through saving in fuel costs. The additional planes meant more exposures for light and ventilation; and the peripheral porches not only sheltered

* Illustrated in John Mead Howells, *Lost Examples of Colonial Architecture,* New York, 1931, Plate 101.

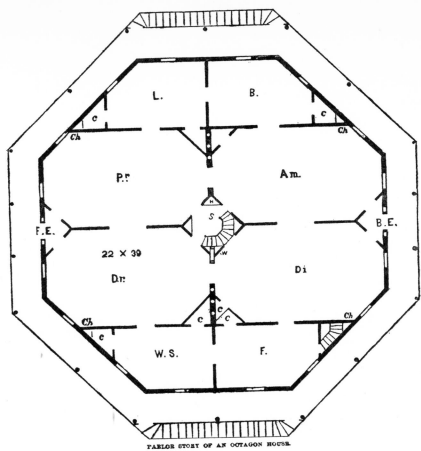

44. *First story floor plan of the Fowler house.*
From Orson Squire Fowler, *A Home for All*, New York, 1854.

the windows and doors, allowing them to remain open in the summertime, even during the most severe rainstorms, but formed a pleasant promenade for exercise in any kind of weather. For a relaxation spot suitable to the temperature one could choose sun or shade at will simply by moving around another bend in the porch. The visual appeal of the architectural pile seemed self-evident to the designer himself, who said: "Beauty and utility are as closely united in architecture as they are throughout all Nature." He declared that "some forms are constitutionally more beautiful than others," and went on to relate the octagonal mass once again to that most nearly perfect solid, the sphere: "the more the angle approaches the circle, the more beautiful. Hence a square house is more beautiful than a triangular one, and an octagonal or duodecagon than either." Fowler had thought of capping his prism with a spheroid dome, but substituted instead a slightly convex roof that caught the rain to fill the tanks for the water supply of the house.

The second part of the title of the Fowler volume referred to the construction system employed in his house. While on a lecture tour Orson Squire Fowler had found in Wisconsin the "gravel wall" that he recommended for octagonal building, originated by one Joseph Goodrich in erecting an edifice to house Milton Academy (later Milton

College, in the town of Milton) in 1844. The walls were composed of lime, coarse gravel, and sand, applied in the manner of poured concrete. Adapted to all kinds of buildings in the neighborhood (including a six-sided residence for the inventor), Fowler reported that walls of this construction were "as hard as stone itself, and harder than brick walls." It was a system made to order for polygonal buildings inasmuch as its plasticity made no problem of various obtuse angles which squared masonry blocks had to be specially shaped to produce. Fowler was as daring in his recognition of new materials as he was in the use of unorthodox forms.

His Fishkill house enclosed four large elongated octagonal interiors on the main floor, the dining and living rooms that could be thrown together to accommodate a large party, the combined area extending almost forty-five by eighty feet. The left-over spaces were anterooms, vestibules, and a stairhall in the exact center, which ascended through the house to the belvedere on top, whence it derived its light. In this respect the plan resembled that of the column house of M. de Monville at Le Désert de Retz. During the hot months the stairwell functioned as a ventilator on the principle of a chimney, drawing fresh air into the rooms below through the windows; and in cold weather persons entered the house on the lowest or service floor and mounted the steps to the main level without causing drafts by opening and shutting outside doors here. Heat came from a furnace rather than from fireplaces in the rooms; and among other up-to-the-minute conveniences were waterclosets and baths on the upper floors, with hot and cold running water. Gas was piped throughout for illumination. It was perhaps the most modern house in America in its day.

Technological advances are blessings only so long as they continue to operate smoothly, and when they fail they can become real menaces. So it was in the Fishkill house. Fowler and his family occupied their octagon less than five years, being forced to vacate due to seepage from a cesspool threatening them with typhoid. From this moment the house was referred to as "Fowler's Folly," until it met with an explosive end upon being dynamited in 1897, the means of disposing of the house a final tribute to the solidity of its construction.

THE OCTAGON MODE

ORSON Squire Fowler's ninety-six-page book, *A Home for All; or, The Gravel Wall and Octagon Mode of Building*, first printed in 1848, was reprinted in 1849, 1850,

45. The Octagon House at Irvington-on-Hudson, New York.

and 1851, and was enlarged to twice its original size in 1853, issued at least four times by the author's concern and once later by his partner alone. Fowleresque schemes found their way into a number of other contemporary books on architecture.* The octagon, therefore, was given ample publicity and wide circulation, with the result that

---

    * Zephaniah Baker, *The Cottage Builder's Manual*, Worcester, 1856, pp. 164–68, and *Modern House Builder*, Boston, 1857, pp. 164–68; John Bullock, *The American Cottage Builder*, New York, 1854, pp. 192–94, 239–41, plates opp. 313, 317, 319; Charles P. Dwight, *The Economic Cottage Builder*, Buffalo, 1856, pp. 44–47, 70–73; Daniel H. Jacques, *The House*, New York (Fowler and Wells), 1859, pp. 47, 83, 124; Samuel Sloan, *The Model Architect*, Philadelphia, 1856, Vol. II, Design 49, and *Homestead Architecture*, Philadelphia, 1861, Design I (Longwood). From Walter Creese, "Fowler and the Domestic Octagon," *Art Bulletin*, June 1946, p. /89/, footnote 6.

eight-cornered houses sprang up all over the country.* Their density was greatest in the picturesque valley of the Hudson River (direct influence of Fowler), in intellectual Massachusetts, and in the homeland of the gravel wall, Wisconsin. At Milton, Wisconsin, the aforementioned Joseph Goodrich's two-story hexagonal house was built in 1845—three years prior to the publication of the Fowler book—so that *A Home for All* here only added sanction to an already established precedent.

The house outstanding because of its bizarre form is the one built by Philip Armour about 1860 at Irvington-on-Hudson, New York. It stands midway between the river and the post road, commanding a fifteen-mile vista across the Tappan Zee and the Palisades. Its unusual effect is due to an elaborate encircling porch and a cupola-on-bonnet superstructure added by Joseph Stiver, who owned the house following the Civil War. Stiver was an importer of teas, and it is said that his trade with India and China was memorialized in the bulging roof mass reminiscent of the Taj Mahal, and in the pagoda-like concave spire of the lantern. The overall shape is something like that of a Nepalese stupa. The house also bears affinities to the then-popular style of the French Second Empire, an eclectic baroque, particularly in the Mansard roof. The irony is that this roof turned out to be a caricature of what Fowler contemplated installing on his own home, thirty-five miles due north at Fishkill. Like the latter the house at Irvington features a central stairhall giving access to the principal rooms, in winter serving as a distributor of heat from the basement furnace. The brick outer walls are encased in wood. The porch is said to have cost $26,000. It has fifty-six posts in sets of twos and threes, between which are railings of cast ironwork, the principal motif in each bay a circular plaque with a profile dog's head in high relief, inscribed "Prince." The house has been nicknamed by various wags "an arrested carrousel," "a magnificent monstrosity," and "a pastry chef's nightmare."† At present the place serves as home for Carl Carmer, author of *The Hudson*, in the *Rivers of America* series, and of many other well known writings.

Matching the Irvington house for picturesque effect was the contemporary Longwood at Natchez, which has been discussed, a larger building, more complex of plan,

* A list of 115 known examples compiled a decade ago gives the following distribution: California, 3; Connecticut, 6; District of Columbia, 3; Illinois, 4; Indiana, 1; Iowa, 1; Maine, 7; Maryland, 1; Massachusetts, 21; Michigan, 3; Minnesota, 2; New Hampshire, 5; New York, 25; Ohio, 4; Oregon, 2; Rhode Island, 1; Vermont, 1; Virginia, 1; Wisconsin, 19. (*Ibid.*, p. 100, footnote 80) Except for two examples (Maryland and Virginia), this list omits octagons in the Southern states, the Creese article being published conjointly with the author's "Some Octagonal Forms in Southern Architecture," *Art Bulletin*, June 1946, pp. 103–11. Pennsylvania, New Jersey, and Kansas also contain examples not included. A recent book on polygonal and circular buildings in America is Carl F. Schmidt, *The Octagon Fad*, Scottsville, New York, 1958.

† The *New York Times*, 22 May 1951, p. 33.

and more thoroughly Oriental in its use of forms. Usually, octagonal houses were a good deal more simple than these last two, following the ideals of their chief protagonist, but which often came to be attributed to the respective builder as original on his part. For instance, the niece of Orlo Shattuck, who constructed an octagonal domicile at Covert, Michigan, about 1889, reports that "Uncle Orlo had a theory that there was less wall space in a round-shaped than a rectangular house."* A man in Yonkers built an octagon in order that his crippled wife might get from one part of the house to another with the least possible effort. A deaf, mute couple erected one at Geneva, New York, possibly having in mind the ease of communication by sign language where all the rooms opened into a common central hall. Similar rational purposes seem to have been behind most of the octagons.

In remote sections of the country the theory prompting the use of the polygon was seldom suspected—much less understood—by persons witnessing the houses. To these people with rectangular minds the obtuse corner seemed absurd. Thus opinionated the townspeople came to ridicule when a cabinetmaker of Columbus, Georgia, began to build a compact, single-story front addition to his existing, twenty-year-old house in 1853, and the new portion was eight sided. An experienced cabinetmaker like Mr. May (for that was his name) would understand how to fit together all the angles properly, and so fashioned the entire structure of wood. It contained four rooms of hexagon shape arranged around a square central chimney affording a fireplace to each room, with triangular spaces between serving as closets or entries, the front vestibule provided with built-in presses for coats and umbrellas and other rainy-weather paraphernalia. There was a gingerbread gothic entrance porch with clustered colonnettes, and a cresting of iron on the porch and around the chimney, which were typical architectural conceits of the period. These and the odd shape prompted May's ill-mannered neighbors to refer to his handiwork as "May's Folly."

At the farther end of the civilized South of the nineteenth century, on the edge of Texas, in the town of Texarkana, lived an enterprising lumberman styled J. H. Draughan, who managed his affairs inside an eight-sided office building—thereby indicating himself a disciple of the octagon mode. It was in 1884, when Texarkana was still in its infancy, that Mr. Draughan entered into a little game of chance, made possible by a lowly deck of cards. Stakes mounted, and Lady Luck smiled upon the gentleman of the timber trade by directing his way a sizeable accumulation of lucre. It was sufficient to finance a building venture, and to this endeavor it was applied. The result was a two-storied house, the plan of which commemorated the configura-

* AP release, January 1955.

46. *May's Folly, Columbus, Georgia.*

47. *Draughan's Folly, Texarkana, Texas.*

48. The ace-of-clubs plan of Draughan's Folly.

tion of an ace of clubs, having a trefoil of living rooms (separated by square passage-ways) grouped around a rotunda stair-hall, the dining room and service wing constituting the stem of the club. The living rooms were octagons in which not even fireplaces were allowed to interfere with their regularity, heat being provided by iron stoves set up only when the temperature warranted their use and taken down immediately afterwards. Eight-cornered chimneys, and a similar-shaped cupola lighting the stair well, rose above the roof line. There was some external Italianate décor, in the bracketed cornices, quoins at the corners, hood molds over the windows, and a spidery iron porch. Draughan's clustered octagon was erected on a terrace high above the street, elevated still higher by a basement story that was mostly above ground level. It is perhaps worth mentioning that Draughan's *chef d'oeuvre* was not the first domestic establishment in the world built in the shape of the ace of clubs, Captain Henry Roebuck having previously built a castle based on this scheme at Bath, England. In spite of the fact that Draughan disposed of his trump at a nice profit, the citizenry of Texarkana—as expected—dubbed it "Draughan's Folly"!

HEXAGON HOUSE

THE APEX of nineteenth-century polygonalism in America was attained in a town designated on the map Mineral Wells, a watering place about forty miles west of Fort Worth, Texas. The man responsible for the construction in question was David

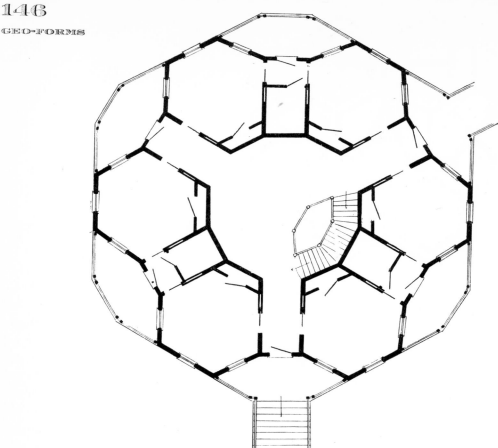

49. *Floor plan of principal floor of Hexagon House, Mineral Wells, Texas.*

G. Galbraith, whose remarkable creation was completed and opened to the public on 6 December 1897.* The building was known as the "Hexagon," which title would have been more explicit in plural form, because, like the ace-of-clubs house at the east border of the state, the Mineral Wells hotel (for that is what it was) consisted of a number of polygon rooms grouped around a central lobby.

The "Hexagon" was not actually six but twelve-sided. The duodecagon mode had grown out of the octagon mode. One of Orson Squire Fowler's followers, by name Zephaniah Baker, built at Dudley, Massachusetts, a home with a dozen sides, and advocated this form in his book, *The Cottage Builder's Manual*, which was published at Worcester in 1856. The circle and the duodecagon divide more favorably for dwellings than the octagon, he contended. A number of twelve- and sixteen-sided houses sprang up in the vicinity of Baker's immediate sphere of influence. Across from Albany, New York, the Greenbush Railway Station of the Civil War period was twelve faced.† Thus, there were East Coast antecedents to the Mineral Wells "Hexagon."

* The author is indebted to the builder's daughter, Mrs. Ann Meriwether, present proprietress of the building, for information contained herein furnished during an interview at a visit to the Hexagon on 17 March 1954, and in subsequent correspondence. Recently Mrs. Meriwether has published an illustrated booklet, *The Hexagon House Story.*

† Illustrated in Benson J. Lossing, *The Hudson,* New York, 1866, p. 139.

50. Hexagon House cipher.

The plan of the building shows the justification for its name, the guest room units being regular hexagons, separated by rectangles that alternate as hallways and bathrooms connected to each suite of two chambers, with a shallow, prismatic porch set in the recesses between the rooms. Such was the arrangement of the first and second floors. A similar scheme was repeated in Galbraith's own apartment on the ground floor; and a circle of small, single rooms on the third floor encompassed the rotunda penetrated by the stair well. The plan, resembling the pattern of a snowflake or a star, bore affinities to the layout of the Star Castle at Prague erected in the mid fifteenth century by George of Podiebrad for Ferdinand II and his successor, Rudolph II. The Bohemian castle was made up of six bastion-like arms, each housing a lozenge-shaped room—one serving as stairhall—with passages between the lozenges opening into the circular innermost court. By eliminating the points of the star the plan of the American hotel avoided acute angles inside the rooms. David Galbraith claimed inspiration from the honeycomb, and used the seven letters of the word "hexagon" inscribed in a honeycomb design on his letterhead, as well as stamped in the iron threshold at the south door, etched in the glass of the Oak Avenue entrance, and a similar pattern executed in cut stonework bounding a small garden in the corner of the yard, where blossomed American Beauty and Marshall Neil roses. The tables in the dining room were hexagonal, and the Reed and Barton silverware was specially imprinted with a hexagon device crisscrossed by diagonals from the corners.

The resort building is built of wood above the stone basement level. The startling external feature is the double row of gables capping the third-floor bedrooms and the fourth-floor belvedere, suggesting somewhat the duplication of gables seen on a Siamese temple. The six-sided house at Milton, Wisconsin (mentioned in the two preceding sections), constructed by Joseph Goodrich, is said originally to have had six false gables with a mock chimney at each peak, the real roof behind concave for collecting the rainwater.* Of interest is the fact that the Milton house was remodeled for an inn, becoming three stories, and acquiring a long, two-storied wing, both blocks covered by flat roofs with projecting eaves.

* Julius P. Bolivar McCabe, *Gazette* (Janesville, Wisconsin), 24 January 1846.

51. *Hexagon House (with dining-room pavilion to the right).*
After an old engraving.

Born in or near Knoxville, Tennessee, in 1855, while a young boy David Galbraith had gone with his family to live on a farm near Carthage, in western Illinois, not too great a distance from Milton, which is only about twenty miles from the Illinois border. Perhaps Galbraith saw the Wisconsin building; its prismatic shape, former

pseudo-gables, and its conversion into a hotel qualify it to have served as prototype for Hexagon House.

David went West around 1880, and with his brother Jim settled on a ranch in Lynn and Garza counties in northwest Texas. He married in 1894 and moved to Mineral

Wells the following year. The symbol of the Lone Star State in latticework was inserted in each of the twelve larger gables of the hotel opened in 1897. The delicacy of the trim belies the boldness of the plan of Hexagon House. The protruding polygon-shaped guest rooms provided extra exposures to light and fresh air, which are as important to maintaining good health as curative waters are to restoring it. Pride was taken in the dining room, housed in a separate rectangular stone structure connected to the first floor of the hotel proper by a passarelle. Here was installed an early ice plant as part of the up-to-date culinary equipment. Here, too, (in the basement of the dining-room pavilion) was a steam plant, the steam used for heat and laundry; and hot mineral water was piped to the baths in each suite. The building also was equipped with the first electric lights in the area. One notes on the plan that the principal interior doors were made to slide back into pockets in the wall to conserve floor and wall space. Handsplit cypress shingles originally covered the roofs, and the woodwork was fashioned from heart of pine. Minton tiles were laid on the basement floor. The last element of Hexagon House to be constructed was the staircase, which was begun at the top and built downward. This factor is indeed significant, making Hexagon House quite unique in that the structure went up and then came down, and after going up and coming down the building stood completed.

8

THE

BUBBLES

TWENTY miles south of Cape Cod lies an island significantly shaped like the silhouette of a spouting whale. It is fourteen miles long. The Indians called it Canopache, "Place of Peace," or Nanticut, the "Far Away Land"; and today it is called Nantucket, which name also is applied to the principal town, located on the north harbor, as well as to the sound separating the island from the cape, bounded on the west by another island, Martha's Vineyard. Nantucket was included in the royal grant to the Plymouth Company in 1621, and, about forty years later, a little before New Amsterdam passed into the hands of the English, the island was ceded to the Province of New York. In 1690 it became part of Massachusetts, and so it has remained ever since. Thomas Mayhew purchased Nantucket in 1641, then, at the end of the following decade, divided his holding up into ten tracts and sold all but one, which he retained for himself. The early settlers engaged in agriculture, sheep raising, and fishing, but when the farmlands were exhausted they turned to the industry for which Nantucket became famous—whaling. Before the Revolution whale oil was exported directly to England in Nantucket vessels. Early in the nineteenth century a rival in whaling arose in the town of New Bedford, with which Nantucket shares the spotlight in Herman Melville's *Moby Dick,* first published in 1851. Meanwhile, shipbuilding and nail and wool manufacturing developed on the island to bring in new sources of revenue, so that during the second quarter of the century Nantucket ranked third among the leading commercial centers of Massachusetts. Afterwards, "the little gray town by the sea" stopped growing in every respect but charm; and now it attracts that curious species of American mainlanders on vacation referred to by the natives as "off-islanders."

Nantucket does not provide an impressive list of wonders to behold. The off-islanders are fascinated by the main cobblestone street of the town; they visit the museum in the

52. Chadwick's Folly, Squam Head, Nantucket.

old Quaker meeting house, view the homes that whaling produced, of course go to see the most ancient house—that of Jethro Coffin, built in 1686 on Sunset Hill—and the old mill dating from 1746. In general they are content with viewing the unspoiled topography and unassuming landmarks, and are transported by the sound of quaint names: Polpis, Wauwinet, Miacomet, Quidnet, Monomoy, Siasconset, Quaise, and Shawkemo. Wauwinet is located on the narrow waist of land joined to the crescent that embraces the harbor with its western extremity and ends at Great Point (called Sandy Point in the eighteenth century) on its northern tip, inscribing an arc of about ten miles circumference. A mile below Wauwinet is Squam Head, facing eastwardly the open sea. On the bluff at Squam Head stands an eerie hulk of a house.

The house at Squam Head is weathered gray, clapboarded on the first story and shingled above. It is an L-shaped mass, with bulging bay windows on the sides, and a square, awkward pent strattling the roof. The central doorway and small, balanced windows piercing the entrance front are in the tradition of Cape Cod domestic building that goes back to the seventeenth century; indeed, the house in question is an elaborated version of the Jethro Coffin house erected two centuries earlier. The more recent building was fashioned for a most unusual purpose: to serve as a gambling casino for millionaires whose yachts could be anchored off its wharf. Such was the dream of the builder, and his ownership still clings to the legend told about the house. His name was Chadwick, and constructing the building was his one bold and daring venture; it proved to be his last. Where he obtained his means to carry on construction became a matter of grave concern to the people of Nantucket. This was because Chadwick was employed in the local bank where their money was deposited. Upon investigation it was found that Chadwick's building fund was being self-appropriated from his place of employment. He was seized, convicted, and put away so that naught came of his ambitious scheme, that would have meant such pleasure to the yacht owners whom Chadwick had hoped to relieve of some of their burdensome wealth, even as he had been relieving the bank up to the time he was apprehended.

Most of the openings in Chadwick's Folly are shuttered or boarded up; a few windows are black voids in the silvery walls. The wind whistles through the empty rooms, filling the vacancy of the entertainers' laughter, and the timbers creak and crack, replacing the sound of the skipping balls of the roulettes. In the game of chance the odds were against the bank clerk whose fingers dipped too deeply into his employer's vault, so that his roseate dream enthroned upon the eminence at Squam Head became instead a bleak and colorless spectre perched atop a barren bluff.

WRIGHT'S FOLLY

WE INVADE the realm of commerce once more as we glimpse the creation of another fearless aspirant to a financial empire that deflated prior to realization. Our attention is directed to the Far West, beyond the steamboat houses along the Mississippi, beyond the honeycomb house in Texas, all the way to the Pacific coast. The place is San Francisco; the time, the middle of the nineteenth century; the builder, Stephen Wright.

Early in the 1850's Stephen Wright was one of San Francisco's leading bankers, looking forward to a brilliant future. His bank vault contained a sum amounting to $150,000, deposited there by those who had faith in his surety and integrity. Wright himself felt that these people deserved some visible symbol of his success and opulence, and hit upon the idea of erecting the most magnificent banking house in California.

The building Stephen Wright envisaged had to be substantial and impressive, well steeped in the most distinguished tradition, and yet expressive of the very latest architectural exemplary. Toward this end he engaged the services of the leading designer of San Francisco, Peter Portois, a Belgian by birth, though thoroughly French by training. The building resulting from this happy combination of client and architect turned out to be Portois' most important work.*

Wright's bank was erected on the northwest corner of Jackson and Montgomery streets, midway between the heart of San Francisco's famed contemporary Chinatown (of little consequence at that time) and the International Settlement, a downtown section of the city that was expanding out toward Telegraph Hill. Montgomery was the main street of the financial district. The building was in the palazzo style, that had been enchanting French architects for several hundred years and during the period of Napoleon III was enjoying a fresh resurgence. In America the style was popularized through the designs of Ammi Burnham Young for court and custom houses, post offices, and marine hospitals, built from coast to coast, beginning with Young's assuming the job of Architectural Adviser to the United States Treasury Department in 1842, and becoming Supervising Architect ten years later. Young's custom house in San Francisco, however, was not completed until 1856, after a period of construction lasting two years,† which means that it postdates the design of Peter Portois by several years, making the bank all the more noteworthy in the city overlooking the Golden Gate.

The bank building was seven bays wide on both fronts, and four stories tall. It was crowned by a heavy cornice supported on dentils and immense carved consoles, doubled at either end of a slightly projecting axial pavilion. A parapet, given the treatment of a pedestal, masked the roof. The first-floor walls were rusticated, reduced to a series of square piers, which increased the size of the intervening openings. The French windows on the second floor were hooded, the three centermost consisting of curved pediments set on consoles, the others triangular. On the next floor the windows were capped by cornice sections on consoles; and the fenestration of the top floor was arcuated. Long balconies spanned the street fronts at the three upper levels, giving the

---

* Agnes Foster Buchanan, "Some Early Business Buildings of San Francisco," *Architectural Record*, July 1906, pp. 29–30.

† *A History of Public Buildings under the Control of the Treasury Department*, Washington, 1901, pp. 44–45.

building the appearance of belonging more to New Orleans than to any other American city, though the railings were of delicate wrought iron rather than of cast ironwork, such as overspread many of the buildings of the Crescent City during the decade preceding the Civil War.

Wright's bank was the best example of the Beaux-Arts tradition on the West Coast. For its construction Stephen Wright appropriated most of the moneys left in his

53. *Wright's Folly, San Francisco.*
    After a photograph in the *Architectural Record*, July 1906.

custody. Then came the panic of 1855, and Wright was leveled like many another ill-fated opportunist, retaining only the mockery of his investment to testify to the ignominy of his failure. The building henceforth was called "Wright's Folly," as one would expect. It survived until the Great Earthquake and resulting fire of 18 April 1906 pounced upon San Francisco, consuming the bank along with most other buildings in this section of the city. A gasoline station now occupies the site.

9

MONUMENT
TO THE WEST'S
WILD PAST

SCHIEFFELIN'S TOMBSTONE AND THE OLD COCHISE COUNTY COURTHOUSE

BY ALL rights of natural law Tombstone, Arizona, ought to be a ghost town, like Jerome in the same state farther north. Both communities got their start and attained the boom stage on account of the discovery of minerals, silver at Tombstone and copper at Jerome. When the supply was exhausted Jerome dried up as any decent has-been should. But not Tombstone. In defiance of its name it managed to live on and came to be known as "the town too tough to die."

When Ed Schieffelin first went out to this site prospecting his friends warned him that all he could hope to find would be a tombstone—meaning the Indians would put him under one. Late in 1877 he discovered silver; and remembering his friends' prediction, he founded "Tombstone" here. Within the next few years the town that sprang up became the most important center between El Paso (on the western tip of Texas) and San Francisco.

Tombstone never was a very large community, but it made up for this deficiency in excessive activity, not least of which were shootings. Practically every structure has become historic as the scene of some killing, such as that of Billy the Kid at the Oriental Saloon or of Marshall White at the Bird Cage Theatre. Both of these buildings are located on Allen Street, the main thoroughfare in Tombstone. Running parallel to Allen on the north are Fremont and then Safford streets, and south of Allen is Toughnut. On Toughnut Street one has the feeling of being on the edge of town; and indeed one is. Running crosswise, First to Sixth streets compose a grid plan, intersecting the afore-mentioned streets at right angles. "Hoptown" is the Chinese "quarter" on Second Street between Allen and Fremont, adjacent to the Mountain-Maid Mining Company; and the Mexican "quarter" is a block farther west on First Street. Outside of Tombstone is Boot Hill Graveyard. The grim humor of the place is reflected in the title of the local journal, the *Tombstone Epitaph!*

54. Cochise County Courthouse, Tombstone, Arizona.

One of the oldest public buildings is the Adobe Firehouse, on Toughnut Street, built in 1880 to shelter the one piece of fire-fighting apparatus used by the Tombstone Volunteer Fire Department. A stone's throw away, at Allen and Fifth, the Crystal Palace Saloon of the same year boasts high ceilings and belated Greek-Revival-style pilasters and door enframements. The Bird Cage Theatre, on Allen near Sixth, was built as a variety house and dance hall the following year. Schieffelin Hall, over on Fremont and Fourth, also dating from 1881, distinguished as the largest adobe building in Arizona, if not in the United States, became the most famous establishment for theatricals in the Southwest.

On Fremont Street, cattycornered from Schieffelin Hall, stands the City Hall, constructed in 1882, an eclectic, bracketed mass of two stories, that still houses the city offices. A block northwest, at the intersection of Third and Safford, is situated Saint Paul's Episcopal Church, the earliest Protestant church continuing in use in Arizona.

At the opposite end of Third, facing Toughnut Street, one comes upon the handsomest building in town, a Renaissance Revival edifice of brick and stone, designed by Frank Walker and built by A. J. Ritter the same year as the city hall and church. Two storied, with a belvedere capped by a Mansard roof at the center of a cruciform plan, and having pedimented gables on all sides, the front one emblazoned with the date of erection, the building served as the Cochise County Courthouse until the county seat was moved to Bisbee in 1929. The rear wing housed the jail, at one time or other accommodating many of the famous outlaws of Arizona. After years of vacancy a group of promoters took a lease on the courthouse from the city, with the idea of converting it into a hotel. Toward this end the upper floor was divided into two levels, the windows changed accordingly, and a flimsy structure—locally referred to as the "penthouse"—affixed to the rear of the belvedere on the roof. The hotel project fell through. Recently a group of civic-minded townspeople, united into a body calling itself the Tombstone Restoration Commission, leased the old courthouse for a quarter of a century with additional options, bent upon restoring it to its former grandeur. It is slated to serve as headquarters for the commission and for the Chamber of Commerce, as a public library and a memorial museum of early mining trophies and other Tombstoniana.* As one faces the courthouse, with his back to the town and only bare hills seen rolling away in the distance, the building gives the impression of a lonely outpost dressed in much too much finery for its untamed surroundings.

The jurisdiction of the Restoration Commission extends over all of old Tombstone, which becomes a sort of Williamsburg of the great Southwest, its original buildings persevering as mementos of a dynamic age. With an altitude of 4,500 feet, the sun shining on an average of 344 days out of the year, free from dust and smoke, the spot is unexcelled as a health mecca. Held in October is the annual Helldorado, in which are re-enacted notorious gun fights and the other highlights of Tombstone's racy history, a constant reminder of its slogan that it is the little town "too tough to die"!

---

* Dorothy G. Palmer, "Tombstone Group's Dream of Restoring Historic Structure Nears Realization," *Arizona Daily Star,* 4 September 1955, Sec. A, p. 8.

10

IVORY TOWERS
OF
BABEL

CHICAGO took its name from the savages—an Indian phrase meaning "wild onion river"—and savage it has taken pride in being. Carl Sandburg, born in Illinois, referring to Chicago as "this my city," spoke of it as having "lifted head singing so proud to be alive and coarse and strong and cunning. . . a tall bold slugger set vivid against the little soft cities. . . . Laughing the stormy, husky, brawling laughter of youth; half-naked, sweating, proud to be Hog-butcher, Tool-maker, Stacker of Wheat, Player with Railroads, and Freight-handler to the Nation."* Chicago became and remained the hub of commerce for the Midwest, the gathering place for the devotees of the god Cash, whose worship calls for many unseemly practices. It is only natural that it should have grown up having little in the way of prettiness and refinement.

The accumulation of wealth is impregnated with the desire for display and often breaks out in as much of it as can be afforded. Good taste is seldom the arbitrator here, where more showy factors fight for—and gain—precedence. The wealthy tycoons of Chicago were well equipped to launch their contributions to American structural monstrosities. Potter Palmer is noteworthy for having accepted his full share.

Potter Palmer, a Quaker from Albany County, New York, who had come to Chicago seeking his fortune, attained prominence in the dry-goods business. His was a fine, big store at State and Washington streets; it was six stories tall, crowned with Mansard roofs treated differently on various pavilions, which building he rented to Marshall Field and Levi Leiter in 1868 for a premium of $50,000 a year. Palmer turned to other endeavors, not least of which was the construction of the hotel bearing his name, the Palmer House, that first opened less than two weeks before the devastating conflagration of 8 October 1871, set off by Mrs. Patrick O'Leary's cow, which consumed both the hotel and store. The hotel was rebuilt two years later, and was a sumptuous edifice,

* *Chicago Poems*, 1916. Courtesy Henry Holt & Co., Inc.

55. Palmer Castle, Chicago.

having a dining hall modeled after the Crown Prince's Palace at Potsdam, a parlor in Empire Egyptian style, staircases of carrara marble, and 225 silver dollars embedded in the floor of the barber shop. How could one have achieved a more lucid exhibition of money?

Potter Palmer engaged the Boston architect Henry Ives Cobb to conceive a home suitable to his position and opulence. It was to be larger than any in the Vanderbilt row; and the architect commented that for size it would have no equal in America "among private residences except some two or three Pacific slope houses of the bonanza kings." The Palmer mansion became the most imposing house in Chicago.

The house was built on Lake Shore Drive between Banks and Schiller in 1882, at a cost of $250,000. The walls were of rough brown Wisconsin granite with a lighter limestone trim, creating an agitated surface in both texture and pattern. It was in the castellated style, the main body being of three stories, with tower and turrets of greater height. The walls rose to battlemented parapets, some machicolated as though the baron living within must defend his keep against besieging armed opponents. The window areas, however, were of generous proportions, in contradiction to the other fortress-like features. It was a house of contrasts.

Palmer Castle was meant to provide a suitable background for the builder's wife, the beautiful Bertha Honoré from the homeland of American beauties, Kentucky. From the *porte cochère* one entered a five-sided vestibule which opened into the great hall that was octagonal. The reception hall was to the right, with the morning room opposite. The library was to the left, and facing it was the open stairhall, flanked by the parlor and dining room, beyond the last were the conservatory and service rooms. Mrs. Palmer's bedroom on the second floor merits description: "All the woodwork in this sumptuous apartment is in ebony and gold. The wall spaces are painted in oil after Moorish designs...the windows are like those in the palace at Cairo, being entirely of lattice-work. .... At the top of the windows is a Moorish arch of ebony, and in the arch cathedral glass in different shades of orange and lemon. The settees and chairs are covered with Smyrna rugs; the paneled wainscot is of wood cut into geometrical designs and the chandeliers to match are of gold and garnet glass."* The room was indeed an "Oriental dream," the decorations by R. W. Bates of Chicago. Messrs. Herter of New York were given charge over the dining room and hall; the mosaic floor in the latter was pronounced by that most eminent of American architects, Henry Hobson Richardson, "the handsomest in the country." His comments on the total effect of the house have not been recorded!

* George William Sheldon, *Artistic Country Seats*, New York, 1886, Vol. I, p. /195/.

As it cost more than his former dry-goods store to construct and decorate, and brought in no returns, Potter Palmer during the spring of 1883 set his heart on selling his castle to some more courageous Chicago millionaire. But Palmer found no one willing and able to purchase the building, and met the situation by manipulating a number of clever deals in North Side real estate, which increased his resources, and found consolation in the compliments his wife received on her Louis XIV drawing room.* A trained ear was required to hear only the favorable comments while ignoring the abuses vociferated against the house. Both, perhaps, were justified, together indicating that Palmer Castle was a mixture of things that were good and things that were bad. The house no longer is the object of praise or ridicule, having been demolished within the last few years.

LINDEN TOWERS

THE COUNTRY home of James C. Flood that stood in Menlo Park, California, was to the Potter Palmer house as a palace to a castle. It was one of the "two or three Pacific slope houses of the bonanza kings" excelling the Chicago residence in size.

James Clair Flood was of middling height, rather stout, quiet, and not given to having many intimates. He had apprenticed to a carriage maker in New York, before heeding the call to "go West," and sailed via Panama to California with the Rush of 'Forty-nine. He tried his hand at mining, but gave it up and went back to his old profession of making carriages and wagons. Then he teamed up with three other Irishmen, O'Brien, Fair, and Mackay, in a scheme that was to develop into a thriving enterprise. Fair and Mackay were expert silver miners, and struck out for Virginia City, Nevada, prospecting. Flood and O'Brien were the speculators, whose part in the deal was producing the wherewithal to maintain the other pair. This was accomplished by opening a cafe-saloon called the Auction Lunch, where they busied themselves mixing drinks and chowders while their teamsters sought the white metal. When success was achieved, their company, Virginia Consolidated, became a household phrase on the West Coast. They built their own bank in Nevada.

Flood had a financial talent that enabled him to go on and upward alone, the returns from the joint enterprise having provided the springboard to greater heights. He came out phenomenally well in the stock market. Twenty-five years after landing in California he was known everywhere as Flood the Banker, the Bonanza King.

* Wayne Andrews, *Battle for Chicago*, New York, /1946/, p. 111.

56. *Linden Towers, the Flood mansion, Menlo Park, California.*

It was time the King had a court to rule, so Flood made plans to build his palace. The site chosen was on Middlefield Road in fashionable Menlo Park, near the southern tip of San Francisco Bay. The house constructed here was enormous, covering almost two acres. The name assigned to it, Linden Towers, recalls that of the High Linden retreat of Ludwig of Bavaria. For vulgar splendor the Flood mansion could be compared better to Ludwig's version of the Palace at Versailles, Herrenchiemsee.

Linden Towers far outstripped Palmer Castle in elaboration and the admixture of styles. It was no compact block of heavy stone, but a vast and rambling pile of wood, its skyline tortured into irregular lacework by towers and chimneys, balustrades, urns and crestings, curved parapets and crowning ornaments. The walls were overspread with pilasters and moldings in twisted and twirled confusion. The windows were made about as different from one another as possible. The porch across the long front of the house gave it the appearance of an expensive Victorian hotel, the illusion furthered by lamp posts scattered about for night illumination. The building represented the quintessence of American eclectic architecture, that medley of styles favored by the nineteenth-century *nouveaux riches* of the New World.

Linden Towers was completed early in 1879. A San Francisco columnist dubbed it "Flood's Wedding Cake." Its reputation improved with distance: *Harper's Weekly* characterized it as "a modification of the Louis Quatorze," which was meant to be complimentary; and *Wasp* called it "the most superb on our continent...no royal or ducal house in Europe excels it."*

The appurtenances were as dazzling as the house itself. The stable provided luxurious quarters for twenty horses, its floor kept as highly polished as that of a ballroom. There was a large domed and vaulted conservatory near the mansion. The gardens were embellished with statuary and a sixty-foot fountain. An artificial lake was stocked with game fish. The broad sweep of lawn appeared endless, so that the owner of the estate felt tremendous importance over being lord and master of all he surveyed from his ginger towers.

The Floods' moving to Menlo Park brought up quite a problem for the older inhabitants: was it proper to call upon the former saloon keeper whose present wealth and well appointed palace made acquaintance so desirable? The matter was resolved with the invitation extended to General Grant to come to Linden Towers for luncheon. His acceptance and presence there affixed the seal of approval, only his partaking of such quantities of delicacies laid out by Mrs. Flood, which curbed his appetite at the homes of established socialites visited later the same day, was viewed with temporary

* Marion Randall Parsons, *Old California Houses*, Berkeley, 1952, pp. 115–16, 118.

indignation and disappointment. That the general would not stuff himself on the first and best food offered to him was, perhaps, taking too much for granted.

Linden Towers has passed into the realm of memory along with the bonanza luncheon through which the Floods took their place in the social world of California.

THE WINCHESTER MYSTERY HOUSE

"IF A MAN make a better mouse-trap than his neighbor...the world will make a beaten path to his door."

Now everyone knows that a mousetrap is a rather minor implement of destruction, and to say something pithy in these times you have to talk about atomic or hydrogen weapons, or at least an instrument with gunpowder in it. And so I offer the following paraphrase of Mr. Emerson's remark by way of introduction to this section: "If a man make a better blunderbuss than his competitors, the world will drive out in droves to gape at the mansion his wife has erected with his money!" One notes the separation of domicile from place of business of the modern inventor; and in this version it is inferred that the product is selling well, though the public is primarily concerned with what the returns have been spent on—by the inventor's marriage partner. Here it is the residence that captivates our undivided interest.

The paraphrase is aimed at the Sarah L. Winchester house located a few miles west of San Jose, California, a building that was under process of construction for over a third of a century, during which time it sprawled out over an area of six acres. Best described as something like a little village of odd, connected houses (all built for a single tenant), such an extensive pile obviously cost a great deal of money; and so our story properly begins with the acquisition of the wealth that made the fantasy possible.

Born in Boston, a city traditionally famous for enterprising businessmen, Oliver Fisher Winchester (the father-in-law of Sarah L. Winchester) first saw the light of day on 30 November 1810. During the next twenty years the light of day witnessed him in the roles of farm-hand, carpenter and joiner's apprentice, and a clerk. It was the clothing business that appealed to him most, especially the manufacturing end of it, and in 1848 he took out a patent on a new method for making shirts. Two years later he had obtained his own factory in New Haven and was well on his way to wealth.

57. Detail of the main entrance and porte-cochère of the Winchester house, San Jose, California.

58. Panorama view over the rear court of the Winchester house.

Fame and greater fortune came through another undertaking. In his adopted city, New Haven, Oliver Winchester began to acquire stock in the Volcanic Repeating Arms Company, and by 1856 he had become its principal owner. The following year he reorganized the company with himself as president, and its name was changed to the New Haven Arms Company, later called the Winchester Repeating Arms Company.

The "Winchester" rifle did not come into being overnight. It was the result of many improvements. The company had inherited the repeating-rifle inventions of Jennings, Horace Smith, D. B. Wesson, and Tyler Henry; the last served as superintendent of the factory and developed a new rim-fire copper cartridge, which easily put the New

Haven product in first place among all others during the Civil War period. Soon after the war Winchester purchased the patent taken out by Nelson King for loading the magazine through a gate in the frame; and the incorporation of this device resulted in the full-blown Winchester rifle.* Sales skyrocketed; and Winchester's affluence was assured.

Old Oliver passed on in 1880; and our attention comes to focus upon the widowed wife of Oliver's son, William Wirt Winchester, as the next important custodian of the Winchester fortune. We find Sarah L. out in California where, six miles from San

* *Dictionary of American Biography*, Vol. XX, New York, 1943, p. 379.

Jose, she purchased a hundred-acre farm, on which was begun an elaborate house that was about ready for occupancy in 1886. The owner, the aforementioned Sarah, did not care for the main cupola, and so it was pulled down and rebuilt. The second cupola did not strike her as right either, and so it, too, was replaced. The third met the fate of its predecessors, and so did the fourth, fifth, sixth, and so on down to the sixteenth, which was allowed to remain. But building operations continued. Sarah believed that when her house would be completed she would die; and so she went on adding room onto room and section onto section, until the result took on the strangest conglomerate quality one could conceive.

"The first view of the house fills one with surprise," reported a visitor during the mid 1890's. "You mechanically rub your eyes to assure yourself that the number of turrets is not an illusion, they are so fantastic and dreamlike."* Mrs. Winchester lived alone with a niece in the great residence and allowed only a few persons to enter the ever-growing sanctum sanctorum. She was described as being shrewd in business, "and socially very exclusive."

Sarah Winchester was a practicing spiritualist, and one of the numerous rooms in the upper part of the house was lined with white satin for the express purpose of functioning as a spirit chamber. Here she welcomed visitors from the other world more heartily than ever was known in her reception room; and who can deny that they must have been a much more interesting and diversified crowd than normally comes in through the front door? Anyway, that was the way she wanted it, and she could well afford to indulge her peculiarities.

The house was pretty much self-sufficient. It had its own heating, lighting, water, and sewage systems. A crew of sixteen carpenters was kept constantly employed; and when they were not making alterations and changes they were forging ahead creating new wings. The additions mushroomed out at the back and sides without rhyme or reason. The house finally included 160 rooms, with a couple of thousand doors and many times that many windows. Blind chimneys, false doors, lanterns and skylights over solid roofs, stairs that led nowhere, trap doors, secret passageways—all were included in the distending domicile.

Expense being no item, one finds gold and silver chandeliers, art glass windows and doors, and the use of rare tropical woods for interior paneling. As soon as a suite was completed it was fully furnished, and then it was seldom entered. Storage rooms were kept filled with every conceivable kind of appliance and furnishing for future

* "Superstition in Building," *American Architect and Building News,* 8 February 1896, p. 68. From the *San Francisco Examiner.*

installation. Conveniences were given as much consideration as luxuries: gas lights were devised to be turned on or off by pressing a button, window shutters could be closed or opened by turning a crank, and down in the laundry corrugated wash boards and soap trays were molded into the forms of the porcelain tubs.

There were thirteen bathrooms, some with glass and some with screen doors. Most of the forty staircases had thirteen steps. Chandeliers were made with thirteen lights; and many rooms were provided with thirteen windows, and ceilings with thirteen panels. Work on the expanding house continued for thirty-six years, or until the death of Mrs. Winchester in 1922. Then all came suddenly to a halt. The house became still. Finally it entered a new career. Halls that had echoed only to hammer, sawtooth, and nail began to reverberate to sounds of visitors' shuffling feet. These visitors enter not through the front doors, valued at $2,000, nor through the white-lined chamber of the shades; but far up the driveway they filter in through a rear entrance to the house, wandering from room to room, mounting the stairs, and crowding onto each elevated loggia, to peer with amazement at each turning, railing and molding that had kept sixteen carpenters occupied for three dozen years.

11

CEREAL AND
PACHYDERM
ARCHITECTURE

THE IMPRESSIVENESS of masonry monuments and increased use of other materials accompanying the gradual depletion of the world's timber supply prompt us to forget that the primary structural substance for man has been plant. The veneration of earliest wood construction in ancient Egypt lingers in the decorative treatment of later stone sanctuaries and burial vaults, known as *serekh*, characterized by vertical paneling; and a similar system determined the design of Mesopotamian ziggurats, such as that dedicated to Marduk at Babylon—the "Tower of Babel," previously illustrated. The pristine employment of timber in India is mirrored in carved beams and posts of antique chaitya halls or Buddhist temples hollowed out of cliffs of solid rock. The parts of the Greek Doric order have been shown to be a carry-over from timber members. The buildings of medieval Europe were mostly built of wood, with the exception of the larger cathedrals, some of which retained wooden vaulting. The structural system of the Far East has persisted in its allegiance to wood, the roof timbers supported on vertical framing, even though encased in thick masonry walls, as at Yüan Ming Yüan. The Japanese house—that has influenced so strongly our own domestic architecture of the present day—is practically a plant creation, combining woods of various kinds, plus straw for thatching and floor mats and bark-paper window panes, held together primarily by wooden pegs, with only a few decorative-headed nails, plastered partitions, and rounded foundation stones supplementing the main materials.

In the area of the United States the aboriginal peoples used saplings bent into hoops and formed into a basket-like framework, tied in place by twisted vines, or else straight poles set into the ground in a circle and coming together at a common apex, to form their half-spherical or cone-shaped tepees. Wood, abundantly provided by virgin forests, was adopted for structural purposes by colonists pouring in from across the Atlantic. The oldest surviving church (the "Old Ship" Meeting House at Hingham,

Massachusetts) and dwellings of New England are frame buildings. The Cape Cod cottage and larger "saltbox" house are traditionally shingled or clapboarded structures. We have seen how stone-intended Greek and gothic forms and polygonal shapes calling for poured concrete often were conceived through the carpenter's craft. Although wood was the ubiquitous American structure element, its surface was seldom left in its natural state, and usually was camouflaged considerably, as at Mount Vernon, where the planks were cut to resemble rusticated blocks and covered with coats of sanded paint to simulate the texture and color of stone.

All races have glorified plants—especially flowers—in their ornament, and in America Benjamin Henry Latrobe originated two new architectural orders for use in the Capitol at Washington, one based on the leaves and blossoms of tobacco, and the other on the ears and tassels of Indian maize, with the column shaft looking like a sheaf of corn stalks, somewhat after the manner of the Egyptian papyrus support. It was perfectly all right to utilize selections from the vegetable kingdom in architectural design so long as one did not allude to the functioning role of plants in construction, according to traditional American thinking.

The Greeks had chosen the pretty, though useless, honeysuckle (anthemion), tulip, and acanthus as models for their decorative motifs, compared to which Latrobe's deliberate selection of crops having economic significance seems a radical artistic departure. In other respects we must concede the choice to be reminiscent of the stylistic decision for the Palace at Brighton—adulating the grandeur of the Eastern empire whence was derived Britain's wealth—yet as thoroughly American as "Lord" Timothy Dexter's image collection of historical personages. Possibly Latrobe would have immortalized "King Cotton," too, had the subject been at all suitable to plastic interpretation in marble or limestone.

The full architectural encomium of an agricultural product was realized in the Midwest during the last decade of the nineteenth century. In the little town of Mitchell— actually the third largest community in southeast South Dakota (population some twelve thousand)—a capatious hall was built in 1892 for shows and public exhibitions, which, despite its more-or-less rectangular overall, manifested some portion of romantic irregularities in the turrets and gables that enlivened the roof. The effect was that of a toy castle of two generations ago, such as would have delighted a puerile Ludwig. But what made the building really distinctive was the fact that its walls were encrusted with squares, circles, lozenges, spirals, and other geometric patterns fashioned of grain, mostly corn of assorted hues, and including flax, oats, millet, and cane. The building became famous throughout the United States as the "Corn Palace."

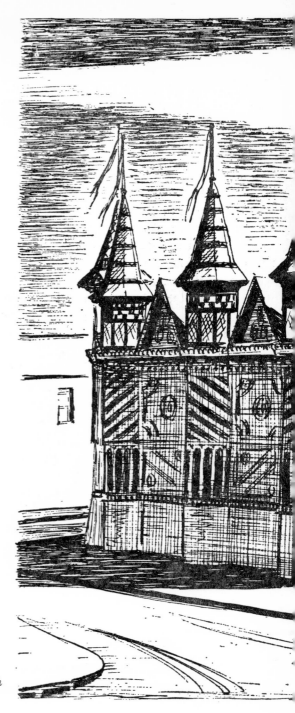

*59. The first Corn Palace (1892), Mitchell, South
Dakota.*

Whether the termites discovered the framework to be as succulent as the birds,
mice, and squirrels found the surfacing, I do not know; but the first Corn Palace was
demolished and a second begun in 1921. The new one had not been completed fifteen
years later when drought necessitated the substitution of evergreen boughs for grain
revetments. At that time the roof had not yet sprouted its flower bed or polychromed

domes and spires, later additions which made the building look like a maharaja's palace rather than a fairytale castle, like its predecessor. The $300,000 building is annually redecorated with about three thousand bushels of corn inlaid into murals depicting cowboys and cowgirls, farmers, Indians, hunters, phases of South Dakota life and the surrounding countryside. Composed of the rich, warm yellows and deep reds

of the ears of grain, running to pale creams and lustrous blacks, the pictures are illuminated at night during the week-long harvest festival each year, at which time vaudeville and musical entertainment are presented in the auditorium seating five thousand spectators. However, the best show is the showplace itself, newly bedecked in its edible

60. Mitchell's second Corn Palace (1921–).

finery. Capitalizing on its cereal façades, a popular magazine recently captioned the palace "The World's Corniest Building."*

* *Life*, 3 January 1955, p. /76/.

THE ELEPHANT HOTELS

NO MORE unusual form of architecture exists than buildings in the shapes of animals. To strain the requirements of human shelter—usually expressed in terms of simple, geometric volumes—to fit inside a zoomorphic enclosure exercises real imagination. Needless to say, although of ancient origin it has not been a common practice to model buildings after animals.

Our thoughts turn to the Sphinx of Giza, fashioned during the third millennium B.C. from a knoll of rock left by the builders of the Great Pyramid nearby. Although it is not, strictly speaking, a building, the Sphinx is of edificial magnitude, measuring 240 feet in length and 66 feet high. The face is a portrait of King Chephren, son of the builder of the Great Pyramid, and himself the builder of the second largest tomb in the Giza group, the entrance ramp of which begins at an open-court building near the paws of the Sphinx, whose duty it was to protect the royal compound. Egyptian drawings of the archaic period indicate that small usable shrines were built in the form of an animal (perhaps Anubis) out of wickerwork or some other light material.*

The famous Horse of Troy was a sort of portable building in equine shape: at least it housed the Greek heroes until they got into the enemy city and succeeded in throwing open the city gates to their confreres waiting outside, a ruse more clever than honorable. The Horse is featured in the story of Helen and the Trojan War of about 1000 B.C. For our purposes the main point of the tale is that the structure made in the likeness of a horse was considered such a prize that the inhabitants of the Asia-Minor city went to great trouble to drag it up to an honored position alongside the temple of their goddess. As it turned out it was to their own destruction; and so the possession of their folly became the folly of their destiny.

In South Asia animal guardians were incorporated in the gateways of cities and fortresses. Parts of a unique survival are to be found in Sigiriya, the Lion Rock, located in the center of the Island of Ceylon. The prominence six hundred feet in height was chosen by the parricide King Kassapa as the site of his citadel in the fifth century, and on the three-acre top he caused to be built the various pavilions of his palace. The entrance was on the north side of the rock, where the protome of a giant lion constructed of brick allowed friendly visitors to pass between its paws to ascend the

---

* Alexander Badawy, "Zoomorphic Shrines in Egypt and India," *Journal of the Society of Architectural Historians*, March 1959, pp. 27–29.

61. Sketch of the Cremona elephant and riders.
After a sketch by Matthew Paris, 1241.

narrow passageway up to the royal residence. The paws are all that remain of the crumbling frontispiece. The idea of the zoomorphic gate had come to Ceylon from India, whence it went also into Indo-China, manifesting itself at Angkor during the twelfth century in gateways emanating elephants, mythical birds, lions, and serpents, crowned by the nine-foot faces of the tutelary Bodhisattva Lokesvara, the pointed superstructure constituting both headdress for the deity and architectural spire.

The animal principally featured in Occidental architectural endeavors is the elephant, whose bulky torso afforded adequate space for rooms. The familiarization of Europe with the elephant was a lengthy process, and one that had to be repeated due to that cultural slump designated the Dark Ages, when no elephant, nor much of anything else, came in. During the Golden Age of Greece, although ivory was known and used, the elephant as a beast had not been introduced. This was left for Alexander, several centuries later. One of his coins shows an equestrian Alexander subduing King Porus of Babylon mounted on an elephant. The young Macedonian entered the city triumphantly in a chariot drawn by elephants, thus initiating a vogue that would be repeated many times in centuries to come. From Alexander the Romans learned the use of elephants in warfare; and that the animal was regarded as almost invincible is indicated by a medal struck by Caesar before he crossed the Rubicon. Caesar is represented in relief, allegorically, as an elephant crushing a serpent senate. The lingering glories of faded classic empire witnessed its last elephant in the personality of Abulabaz, the pachyderm received by Charlemagne from the court of Harun-al-Rashid. After Abulabaz died in 804 none of his tribe was in Europe again until the thirteenth century.

It was Frederick II who acquainted Europe with the elephant once more. When Richard of Cornwall visited Italy in 1241 the jubilant citizens of Cremona brought

62. *Elevation of "L'Éléphant Triomphal," proposed monument to Louis XV.*
From the *American Architect and Building News*, 9 August 1890.

out the prize possession of Frederick's menagerie to honor the visiting dignitary; and an English artist, Matthew Paris, recorded the phenomenon in a little drawing showing the elephant carrying on his back a palisade-type howdah filled with musicians and other revelers, one prodding the animal from behind with a sharp sword, while on the elephant's head sits the mahout clanging a bell. Frederick II revived the classic elephant-triumph when, after vanquishing the Milanese, he entered Cremona in procession, his elephant pulling the captured chariot containing the fettered podesta of Milan.

A step nearer pachyderm architecture was taken when life-size elephant automatons

63. Section of "L'Éléphant Triomphal."

came into being. The precedent may be traced back to a dummy on wheels owned by
Ptolemy, the successor of Alexander in Egypt. After the lapse of many hundreds of
years we hear of a banquet held for Philip of Burgundy during the middle of the fifteenth century, upon which occasion the chief of the Burgundian School of Rhetoric
diverted the company by dressing himself in a nun's garb and riding in on a mechanical elephant to recite a threnodic lament on the dangers threatening the church from
the Turks. A century later Henri II staged his *entrée* into Rouen with several elephant
automatons, which were pronounced so realistic that "even those who had seen live
ones in Africa would not have judged them imitation elephants." They carried on their
backs towers of diverse forms, embellished with banners or urns belching forth flames.
Evidently they were propelled by manpower from the inside.

The elephant became a rather popular motif in art during the sixteenth and seventeenth centuries. Living specimens were owned by Emanuel I of Portugal, Charles V of

Spain, Louis XIII of France, Pope Leo X, and one private citizen, by name Mijnheer Sevender. A noteworthy representation in marble was the almost-life-size elephant supporting a tall Egyptian obelisk on his back, commissioned by Pope Alexander VII of the sculptor Bernini and erected in the Piazza della Minerva in Rome.*

No more spectacular manifestation of elephant inspiration has been conceived than in a contrivance of the Frenchman, M. Ribart, who published his creation in 1758 under title: *Architecture Singulière: l'Éléphant Triomphal, Grand Kiosque, à la Gloire du Roi.* The reigning monarch at that time was Louis XV. M. Ribart proposed his royal tribute to be set at the terminus of some view as from the Tuileries up the Champs Elysées to the *étoile.* It was to be embodied in the form of an elephant standing in repose, bearing a tower bristling with a panoply of arms and banners and capped by a statue of his majesty, the whole magnificently caparisoned and elevated on an arcuated platform giving access through vaulted galleries to the wonderful apartments inside the pachyderm itself. A straight flight of steps—the *Grand Escalier* —led up to the first landing, whence one ascended the spiral staircase within a rustic shaft connecting with the animal's belly. The kitchen and offices were situated in the lower forequarters of the colossus, their windows concealed by a wide necklace ending in a pendant bell hanging in front of the shoulders. Another flight up the staircase led to the bath—in the hind parts. It was elaborately decorated, as were the other superior apartments. The principal interior in front was described as an amphitheatre to be used for balls, performances and as a general assembly room. An alcove raised several steps in the head of the elephant provided a place for the throne of the king, with light streaming in through fenestration incorporated in the headpiece of the trappings. The last great room to the rear was a banqueting hall, the dome of which, following the contours of the elephant's back, was to be treated in the manner of a forest glen, with trees and vines masking its limits, and having a brook encircling the room, incorporating a series of cascades, the water emptying into the bath underneath. A winding path (in reality a narrow stairway) ascended from the dining room to a small card-room over the stairwell. The elephant was supposed to be quenching his thirst, but instead the uplifted end of his snout regurgitated water into a tank, witnessed by a bevy of mermaids. As it happened, M. Ribart's masterpiece never materialized to honor Louis XV nor any other ruler.

Another elephant monument was to have been erected in the square that came into being from the demolition of the Bastille in Paris. After the space had stood bare

* William S. Heckscher, "Bernini's Elephant and Obelisk," *Art Bulletin,* September 1947, pp. 155–82.

64. The Elephant Hotel, Margate City, New Jersey.

65. The Elephant Hotel, Coney Island.
After a photograph taken from the old iron tower brought from the Philadelphia centennial.

for a dozen years Napoleon Bonaparte proposed the construction here of the largest triumphal arch in the world, only the Academy of Fine Arts frowned upon the site and recommended the spot where it was actualized, in the Place de l'Etoile, the location M. Ribart had chosen for his leviathan. A fountain to be cast from the metal of captured Spanish cannon next was suggested, but with no more success than the arch. The matter was put into the hands of an architect by the name of Alavoine, who made fourteen miscellaneous designs before he hit upon that of an elephant, which seems to have won the approbation of the committee. At least a model was made, consisting of a framework of wood and iron covered with plaster, thirty feet long and forty-five feet high. Shown in an old woodcut to have been an elephant less slouchy than M. Ribart's, he carried on his back a crenelated howdah from which hung loose drapery concealing auxiliary supports, and around the base played fountains fed by a pump in the howdah. But the model stage was as far as this scheme got. In its stead was placed the Column of July known to every Paris visitor.

Such grandiosity as that of an Éléphant Triomphal would be out of place in America, but by the very virtue of abandoning the superficial trimmings Americans often were able to bring the essential features to realization. An elephant building exists in America. It is referred to as the Elephant House, or, more usually, as the Elephant Hotel at Margate City, near Atlantic City, New Jersey. No pedestal nor platform supports this elephant, for he is a pleb pedestrian with feet planted firmly on the ground. In the practical American manner he is depicted in a feeding attitude. Summer vacationists have flocked to this section of the Atlantic coast for several generations, and a good percentage still go to view the baggy-kneed landmark. Constructed by James V. Lafferty about 1883, the monster has an overall length of about seventy-five feet, the height to the peak of the original howdah surpassing this measurement by ten feet. Over a million pieces of timber went into the construction of the thing, plus four tons of bolts, bars, and nails, and twelve thousand square feet of tin for covering it —according to the leaflet passed out by the proprietors.

Twin newel stairways are in the hind legs, one for ascent and the other for descent. The interior space is divided up into rooms devoted to the ordinary purposes of a house, including a reception room eighteen feet square, dining room, kitchen, and several bedrooms. Twenty windows are for the admission of light, besides the eighteen-inch portholes that serve for eyes. Staircases to each side of the belly take one to the howdah, where, from an elevation of sixty-five feet, is obtained a wide vista of the sea. The cost of building the elephant is said to have been $38,000.

Lafferty built a similar hotel on Coney Island at about the same time, though the latter one only survived until 1896, in which year the elephant was burned (or, should one say, was cremated?).* The Coney Island construction, billed as the "Elephantine Colossus," was bigger than the one farther down the Atlantic coast, having three complete stories within the torso, the overall height amounting to 122 feet. The forelegs of this jumbo were put to good usage, one accommodating a cigar store and the other a diorama, later one or the other converted into an elevator shaft.† Staircases were in

* Edo McCullough, *Good Old Coney Island*, New York, 1957, pp. 55, 304.
† According to the account of Mr. William Van Cleef of Brooklyn, interviewed 22 October 1957.

J. V. LAFFERTY.
BUILDING.

No. 268,503.   Patented Dec. 5, 1882.

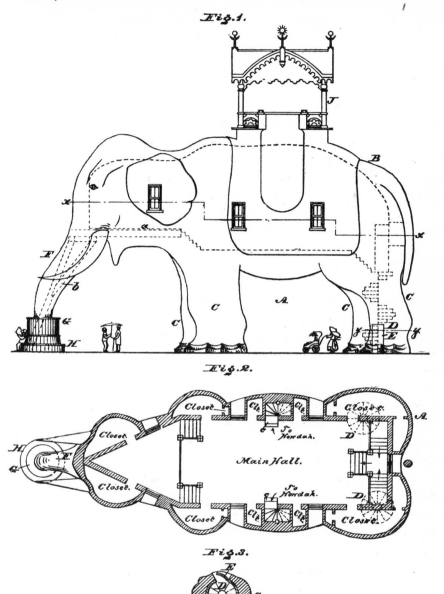

Fig.1.

Fig.2.

Fig.3.

66. *Elevation and plan of the Elephant House.*
From James V. Lafferty's patent, 5 December 1882.

the hind legs. People could engage rooms in any part of the animal's anatomy they wished. The monster was glamorized in a number of contemporary prints, one, dated 1885, showing a turbaned mahout figure (about ten times life-size) in front of the howdah on the pachyderm's back, the elephant standing no farther than his own length from the ocean surf.* In actuality, he stood in a gardened court—as though he were the Kaaba in the Great Mosque at Mecca—the surrounding neighborhood, however, enjoying a none-too-savory reputation. In spite of being much larger than his mate near Atlantic City this elephant had more of the look of a child's plaything about him, appearing somewhat like a much-inflated balloon elephant. His howdah was more elegant than the one in New Jersey.

A patent was taken out on the invention by James V. Lafferty. It was filed 3 June 1882, and granted on December the 5th. The description was accompanied by a diagram representing a side elevation and plan of the "building in the form of an animal, the body of which is floored and divided into rooms, closets, &c., and the legs contain the stairs...said legs being hollow, so as to be of increased strength for properly supporting the body." One wonders that old Mother Nature never thought of the supporting quality of hollow legs; but, on the other hand, how could Mr. Lafferty locate his stairs in them if they weren't? There is only a single large, rectangular room, however, the leftover spaces all portioned off into closets, and even inner-closets. The trunk was a useful member, having a chute inside (marked "F" on plans) for the disposal of "slops, ashes, &c." In the next paragraph we read: "The elevation of the body permits the circulation of air beneath it and removes it from the dampness and moisture of the ground. ... Furthermore, the body is exposed to light and air on all sides, wherefore it provides a healthy and suitable place of occupancy for invalids and others." The inventor did not specify whether he meant physical or mental invalids, but it becomes apparent that the former could never maneuver the winding stairways; and a second glance at the structure itself confirms the supposition that it was constructed exclusively for the latter. Forming a house according to the shape of an elephant seems a mighty roundabout way of exposing rooms to the light and air! How Orson Squire Fowler would have shuddered at this application of his doctrine! The description concludes: "The building may be of the form of any other animal than an elephant, as that of a fish, fowl, etc." So—how about a big *bug house* for the inventor?

---

* Booklet of engravings showing scenes of Coney Island, published by Adolph Wittemann, Leipzig, 1885. Long Island Historical Society.

12

IMPORTATIONS,
INTEGRATIONS,
AND
IMITATIONS

THE ENTHUSIASM over imported styles during the early and middle years of the nineteenth century led naturally to the importation, physically, of actual buildings from across the seas. After all, authenticity—such being desired—could go no further.

We are going to look at two examples of late-nineteenth-century imported houses, one of which had some of its parts come from across the Atlantic, and the other that came in its entirety across the Pacific Ocean.

The first was commissioned by A. D. Fisher and built in Walnut Hills, a suburb of Cincinnati, near where the first log cabin in this vicinity had been constructed eighty years earlier. The Fisher house was in the Swiss chalet idiom, a style that had been gaining momentum in America ever since the publication of Design X, for "A Swiss Cottage," in A. J. Downing's book, *The Architecture of Country Houses,* in 1850. The Swiss manner was less academic than any of the Revival styles, and its use of timber was well suited to the American building supply at that time. Nowhere in Europe, other than in remote mountainous regions, could wood still be used extensively in structural work, but in America forests were plentiful. The chalet, with its widely overhanging eaves and well insulated timber walls, the planks forming its walls carefully grooved and tightly fitted together over splines, and with generous porches, was found to be quite agreeable to the American climate and way of life. The carved and painted peasant designs also caught the American eye.

The progenitor of the Swiss style in Cincinnati was Lucien F. Plympton, an architect of some imagination, who is said to have married a Swiss woman and to have maintained connections in Switzerland. When he was engaged to design the Fisher house it was arranged that the woodwork sheathing the upper floors be produced in Switzerland. In area the Fisher châlet is not large, only about thirty by forty-five feet, exclusive of

67. The A. D. Fisher châlet, Walnut Hills, Cincinnati.

the overhanging service wing on the main-floor level at the rear; but it is two-and-a-half storied in front, and, due to the slope of the lot, four-and-a-half storied in back. The site, even, is reminiscent of the Swiss Alps. A stream is at the foot of the hill at the end of the yard. The striking feature about the house is the seven-foot eaves on all sides supported on tremendous consoles, exquisitely detailed. The banded windows make for pleasantly lighted rooms. The great hall is entered from the front porch (at present enclosed), a staircase winding upward in the right-hand corner to a gallery that encircles an open well, the end wall above the landing devoted to fenestration. On the wall opposite, downstairs, is the fireplace of the living room, an extension of the hall, and expanding into a recess adjoining the front porch. The dining room, with an outdoor balcony beyond, and the service space and kitchen are behind the living-hall, the cooking and eating rooms connected by the pantry-service room supported on brackets that has been mentioned. Upstairs, the master bedroom is across the front of the house, and there were three small chambers besides, one of which has been converted into a second bath room on this floor. The house now is owned and occupied by the Director of the Cincinnati Art Museum. Begun during the 1880's, the Fisher chalet was completed in 1892.

A chalet was built for the World's Columbian Exposition in Chicago during 1892–

93; it was a rustic, log affair that housed the Idaho State Exhibition. A more authentic Alpine house was to be seen in the German Village on the midway, claimed to have come from a Bavarian farm. The unexpected imported buildings at the Chicago Fair were from Farther Asia. There was one from Japan (see Chapter XIII, Part 3), and another that had been the home of a tea planter in Ceylon, presented to the Singhalese

68. *Ceylon Court, Lake Geneva, Wisconsin.*

government by the builder, and then shipped to this country in pieces. As reassembled for the exposition the building was composed of an octagonal pavilion flanked by equally balanced rectangular wings. The central mass was crowned with superimposed pyramidal roofs, and the wings had double-pitched hipped roofs, with cutout designs hanging from the cornices and bristling atop the ridges.

69. The great hall of Ceylon Court.

The Ceylon Building was sold after the close of the fair, and, in 1894, the wooden structure was carted seventy miles northwest to serve once more as a domestic establishment, overlooking Lake Geneva in Wisconsin. In its new role it was considerably altered. The octagon was enlarged into a three-storied mass (a story inserted between each of the upper roofs); and the wings were given two floor levels and placed on cross axes to one another, with an extended porte-cochère at the entrance, and the addition of turrets, and brick and terracotta chimneys, the protome of an elephant protruding from the principal chimney. A plaque below the animal proclaimed this to be "Singhalese Villa," though it was known more generally as "Ceylon Court." It was the John J. Mitchell and later the E. H. Maytag residence.

The house was decorated in lavish taste, many of the furnishing brought from the Far East. The focus of interest is the octagonal hall adorned with intricate carvings in numerous kinds of wood, including teak, satinwood, ebony, mahogany, and cypress. A circular staircase is in the center of the hall, enclosed within a ring of carved posts on which the ceiling beams radiate to perimeter supports, with inlaid friezes between depicting deities and Oriental pageantry. There are six bedrooms in the villa, besides servants' rooms and a dormitory in the tower. On the seventeen-acre grounds are a gate lodge, boat house and garage, and a Chinese bath house by the swimming pool, which last is a modern addition. The house commands a superb view across twelve miles of water. At the time of writing the estate has been on the market for a dozen years, a poignant indication that the day of the great houses in America has just about become a thing of the past.

The twentieth century has witnessed the importation of a number of other buildings to the United States. One of these is a half-timber, sixteenth-century house from Ipswich, Suffolk County, England, added in 1911 to the granite Tudor-style residence built seven years earlier by and for the architect I. N. Phelps Stokes on Round Hill Road near Greenwich, Connecticut. Arthur S. Vernal also brought over parts of an English house for his home at Ossining, New York, about 1913.* And a fourteenth-century Lancashire manor was re-erected in 1925 at Winsor Farms near Richmond, Virginia, owned by T. C. Williams, Jr. William Randolph Hearst imported a Spanish medieval monastery, which recently was rebuilt near Greynolds Park in the northern suburbs of Miami. In the same state supports for an eighty-column arcade in the Ringling Museum at Sarasota (1931) include various European specimens, of fairly uniform size, dating from the eleventh through the sixteenth century. On the grounds of Florida Southern College a Methodist bishop caused to be reassembled a tiny Hindu temple brought from Banaras, having a Garden of Meditation nearby, and a Wishing Pool in front, from which the pennies are collected to supply candles for the Christian altar inside the five-by-nine-foot shrine.

CITADEL OF ALL RELIGIONS

THE GOOD thing about importing houses bodily from foreign lands during the age of American eclecticism was that each house came from a single place, a single country, and upon arrival (at least) each displayed a unified, consistent style. What happened to them afterwards is another matter. The theory behind eclecticism was to borrow from anywhere and everywhere, and combine all elements freely according to one's inclination and taste. The objective seems to have been to arrive at something different, if not at something new. The fallacy was in attempting to push ahead while the vision was directed backwards—obviously making it difficult to see where one was going. Most designers believed that they were combining only harmonious elements;

* *Arts & Decoration*, September 1914, pp. /400/–403.

though today it is rather difficult, usually, to appreciate their admixtures. The modern eye is offended by bizarre accumulation of elements; the mind refuses to assimilate such potpourris of architecture.

The closing decade of the nineteenth century was the hour of triumph of theoretical synthesis. The motive behind the World's Fair in Chicago was to bring together all the different manifestations of various phenomena: the arts, the products of industry, agriculture, and forestry, achievements in science, medicine and invention, and even religion. Religion, of course, would be the last field attaining synthesis, most often having to do with perpetuating beliefs rather than seeking truth. It was recognized that the World's Parliament of Religions, as it was called, would incite considerable interest and curiosity, and so it was decided to hold the meetings outside the fair grounds. The auditorium of the Chicago Art Institute was engaged for the purpose; and announcements sent out to personages everywhere brought in replies from over fifty countries. Some praised the program because it would broaden men's minds; but more favored it because it would provide them with the opportunity of airing their own opinions, and thus bring others (they hoped) into their way of thinking. Another group condemned the idea on the grounds that the parliament would allow heretical teachings to be proclaimed, meaning, of course, teachings other than that to which they themselves subscribed; and they objected to lowering their own particular creed to a level with others. Despite opposition the plan carried.

One of the most colorful figures to step upon the platform of the World's Parliament of Religions was Swami Vivekananda, the disciple of the Indian holy man, Ramakrishna. Vivekananda was referred to as the "Hindu Monk," though he hardly seemed to correspond to the usual concept one has of a monk, appearing "clad in gorgeous red apparel, his bronzed face surmounted with a huge turban of yellow." In contradistinction to his late emaciated teacher, Vivekananda was corpulent, matching better the average Western Victorian of that overstuffed era. He won the hearts of his audience by addressing them as "Sisters and brothers of America"—a greeting establishing confidence no other religious leader had thought of using—but irritated them somewhat when he advised Christian missions to send food and not religion to India, where they already had enough of the latter. It was with varied emotions that the main message of Vivekananda's speech was received. He proclaimed that it was an ancient Hindu principle to recognize all faiths as expressions of truth, and stated that from his earliest boyhood he had repeated a sacred text, spoken daily by millions of Indians, which said that as different streams, having their sources in different places, eventually all mingle their waters in the same sea, so the diverse paths men take

70. Vedanta Center in San Francisco.

through varying religions lead them all to the one Lord. He pictured India as the land of religious toleration, offering asylum to persecuted groups from time immemorial. Vivekananda convinced some of his listeners that Hinduism provided satisfactory answers to vital problems facing the modern Occidental world, where other sectarian religions failed, by virtue of which he began to accumulate a band of followers. These he eventually organized into the Vedanta Society, the title of which refers to the *Vedas*, the oldest documents of Aryan philosophical and religious wisdom.

Vivekananda was succeeded by other swamis from the Ramakrishna Math or Monastery. Vedanta centers sprang up in the larger cities and some of them prospered. The society in San Francisco constructed its own building in 1905 at the southwest corner of Webster and Filbert streets on Russian Hill. The design of the building was the idea of the leader, Swami Trigunatitananda, working with the architect, Joseph

A. Leonard. The main entrance, on Webster Street, was recessed behind Ionic columns *in antis*. Bowed windows and cornices above, and overhanging bay windows on the flank of the frame structure were elements of the Colonial Revival style then popular on the West (as well as East) Coast. Lobated arched windows to the first story on the Filbert Street side of the Center were of Oriental origin. The forms on top were what made the building really unusual, the effect heightened (literally) through the later addition of a third story surrounded by a lacy arcade, the original superstructures raised another ten feet into the air. On the round turret at the corner is a double bulbous dome, balanced by a crenelated parapet on the cylinder over the main entrance. The second projecting bay on the Filbert Street flank is topped by what resembles an octagonal Byzantine melon dome. The third bay is crowned by a cluster of pointed domes, like the upper portion of a Jain temple. The rear wing, which is two storied, features a Mughal-type dome over the doorway leading into the meeting hall. The curious topmost forms symbolize the world's great religions, gathered together upon— as within—the Vedanta edifice. It was the embodiment of Vivekananda's concept of all creeds leading to the one God. It was the Citadel of All Religions, the Reverie of Akbar, the Indian emperor who had conceived the same dream over three centuries earlier, as expressed in words put into the mouth of the humane Indian emperor by Tennyson:

> *"I dreamed*
> *That stone by stone I reared a sacred fane,*
> *A Temple; neither Pagod, Mosque, nor Church,*
> *But loftier, simpler, always open-doored*
> *To every breath from Heaven; and Truth and Peace*
> *And Love and Justice came and dwelt therein."*
>
> AKBAR'S DREAM

THE LEANING TOWER OF NILES

ONE HAS to be slanted in a certain direction to appreciate architectural facsimiles; and one has to be considerably off keel to be steered so far away from the normal course of human behavior as to actually sponsor the building of one. There was a Scotsman, for instance, a Mister McCaig, who completely defied the decorum of frugality for which his nation is famous, by spending some £500,000 erecting a replica of

71. The Leaning Tower of Niles, Illinois.

the Roman Colosseum at Obau, Scotland, presumably out of sentiment over having passed his honeymoon in Rome.* One can conceive of a madman like Ludwig II wanting a copy of palaces belonging to the tyrants whom he idolized—drawing upon the state treasury to have them—but for plebeians to sink their own earnings into reproducing someone else's *folie* is, indeed, a bit unusual. It is more within the range of expectation for them to concoct their own. Slanted, especially, is the person putting up a slanting reproduction, the slanting of which conforms to the slant of the slanted original.

Chicago is a city famous for its towers, not merely for the figurative ivory towers of its enterprising merchants, like Potter Palmer, but for actual sky-piercing constructions. The old Water Tower built in 1869 on the North Side (a neighbor to the Palmer castle) is one of the earlier Chicago oddities of verticality. In gothic style, the stone structure consists of a square base resembling a toy fort, having telescopic turrets at the corners; and on the center was set a second elongated square mass with additional turrets dangling in superposition from its corners, and with an octagonal shaft on axis rising half again as tall as the combined lower forms, terminating in a cluster of turrets and a pointed dome. Chicago was the hotbed for the early skyscraper, notably in the work of William Le Baron Jenney during the 1870's and '80's, and of Holabird and Roche, Burnham and Root, and Sullivan and others during the 1880's and '90's. The towering buildings built by these men had a decided influence upon the architecture that was to follow. The tower toward which we now turn our attention apparently exerted no influence of any kind on anything.

At Niles, a suburb of Chicago, located about a dozen miles northwest of the Loop, an industrialist, by name Robert A. Ilg, built a half-size copy of the well known Leaning Tower of Pisa. The prototype in Italy, a campanile or free-standing bell tower, situated to the rear of the Pisan Cathedral, was built during the late twelfth century, with the small belfry proper on top added in the mid fourteenth century. A round first story encircled by a blind arcade constitutes the basement to six additional floors having open galleries within a ring of thirty columns supporting an equal number of arches at each stage. The building is not a perfect cylinder because of a slight curve to its axis, which came about due to subsidence of the foundations, causing the campanile to lean toward the south. The attempt was made to correct this condition through adding a little height to the columns on the low side as each story was constructed, but the matter became increasingly worse, and at slightly over 150 feet the project came to a standstill. Nothing further was done save for the addition of the small penthouse a century and a half later. Though the tower has a diameter of only

* "Believe It or Not," 7 May 1950.

fifty-two feet, the outermost point of the top cornice—from which Galileo is said to have let fall the objects that proved his theory about solids of different weights falling with the same velocity—overhangs the base some thirteen feet. The tilt increases about .027 inches a year, and it has been recommended that the tower be taken down and rebuilt on a new concrete footing.*

The diminished replica in Greater Chicago was constructed in 1932 for use as a summer home. It has the same number of stories as the Pisan tower, but, although proportionally smaller and in scale, has fewer columns per floor. A wrought-iron railing, not found on the original campanile, joins the supports of the summer-house. The stairways, instead of being built inside the wall, as in the prototype, rise at the high side of the open galleries, which means that one has to circumambulate all lower stages to get to the upper stories. What a precarious feeling one would have gotten had the stairs been placed on the lower side, where the mounting process would have taken a person out over a void! The Niles tower differs from the Pisa tower in that the ground floor is flat with the ground and not sloping. Trees growing on the property, that goes by the name of Ilgair Park, take away from the dramatic austerity produced by the absence of planting on the cathedral lot at Pisa. An extraneous note, though also Italian, is introduced by placing the American tower by the side of a pool, with decorated posts for tying up Venetian gondolas at the water's edge, and small arched bridges connecting a series of artificial islets.

In 1949 the builder announced that he was " 'plumb tired' of leaning," bid goodbye to the Leaning Tower and moved his family to California, where he obtained a house in which he could live on the level.†

* The *New York Times*, 18 April 1956, p. 33.
† The *Lexington Leader*, 15 November 1949, p. 2.

13

SHODDY FOLLIES:
ORIGINALS OF
THE TWENTIETH
CENTURY

THE REMARKABLE that is not pretentious is more remarkable than that which is. Though Americans have gloried in pretentiousness they have not often been able to afford much of it. The remarkable things that they have produced have had a tendency to be comparatively unpretentious, and especially unpretentious is the group of structures which we are now going to consider.

Builders today pride themselves on using new materials. Usually this involves some far-fetched composition or trick of construction, whereby the builder demonstrates his virtuosity. At best this is an affectation. But sometimes the use of unorthodox materials springs honestly from convenience or necessity; the uniqueness of the final effect is incidental, the builder having preferred that his house have a more normal appearance. It is especially true where the structural material has base associations.

There is a saying about people who live in glass houses not throwing stones. The people living in glass houses often live in them because they have no stones to throw, else they would have used the stones for house building, instead of using glass, which, for one reason or another, was more readily available.

Out in the great American desert, where the land is rich in minerals, but not in much of anything else, a miner, one William F. Peck, set his mind upon building a house for his wife, two small children, and himself. He was at Tonopah, near the western boundary of Nevada, on a latitude with San Francisco. There was not a tree within sixty miles. During his spare time he managed to construct a two-room house measuring sixteen by twenty feet in area, with an eight-foot ceiling. Its walls were composed of empty beer bottles, and it is reported that the Pecks found their house "exceedingly comfortable at all times."* It was completed and occupied in October of 1902.

In the ghost town of Rhyolite, Nevada, about eighty miles south of Tonopah and near

* *American Architect & Building News*, 28 November 1903, p. 72.

72. Bottle house in the ghost city of Rhyolite, Nevada.

to Daylight Pass, which leads into Death Valley, under similar circumstances another house was constructed three years later. This one was bigger and built of liquor instead of beer bottles, a total of fifty thousand incorporated into its walls. It was Tom Kelley's house, boasting the refinements of a little jigsaw decoration on the gables and turned wooden posts and railing to the porch. This is one house in a ghost town that once claimed an undeniably tangible assortment of spirits within.

Bottle house construction is still practiced. On Lake Magdalene, near Tampa, Florida, Thad Clark built a five-room residence out of ten thousand slightly nicked milk bottles. The house has a nearly flat roof. It is square and severe, the form relieved only by a few openings and an external chimney shaft. Another contemporary example is at Hillsville among the Appalachian Mountains in southern Virginia. Measuring twenty-four by seventeen feet, the walls contain a great variety of bottles ranging in size from twelve ounces to a gallon, the larger ones placed below and graded smaller towards the top. The builder, John W. Hope, was a pharmacist, in the dispensation of whose professional duties he automatically supplied himself with building blocks—or building bottles. In other words, he managed to build up his business and home simultaneously.

What better folly is there than to live in a bottle? And the next best thing is to dwell in a house *of* bottles—beer, whiskey, milk, or medicine. You, too, can do it, if you start saving whatever kind of bottle you specialize in partaking the contents of, for your future bottle home.

CARVILLES, U. S. A.

THE LIGHTWEIGHT tepee, that became the typical home of the Plains Indians after their capture and domestication of wild horses whose ancestors had escaped from the Spanish *conquistadores* of Mexico and our own Southwest, which brought about a change of life from that of settled agrarians to roving nomads, was prophetic of the later dwellings of the white people who supplanted the bronzed natives on this continent. Its obvious manifestation was the portable house that had come into being by the 1850's. Even the permanent American home appeared to the English novelist, Charles Dickens, on his visit to this country shortly before, as something put up just for the weekend and was to be taken down first thing Monday morning.* The automobile-trailer craze a century later was a resurgence of the American favoring of minimum shelter. Peoples of the Old World have come to look upon America as a nation addicted to yurts, and their observation is not without some justification, as will be shown through a movement that flowered around 1900.

The adoption of self-powered trams in place of horse-drawn railcars for city public transportation was accompanied by the problem of what to do with the old rolling stock. One assumes the horses found employment pulling milk and brewery wagons, and imagines them coming automatically to a halt whenever they saw any of their former customers, expecting them to climb aboard. The cars, however, were provided with no such role of participating in the throbbing life of the city. For the time being it looked as though they were of no further usefulness to mankind.

But Americans have a way of making the discarded into the highly regarded, and so it was when their ingenuity was brought to bear upon the old horse cars. It is hard to say where the phenomenon started, and whether the idea was taken from place to place or was spontaneously conceived everywhere at once, prompted by the ubiquitous situation. The cars came to fare better than the horses who had pulled them, being given a retirement-vacation for the rest of their existence.

A congregation of cars taken from the streets of New York City was transported to a spot near Bridgeport, Connecticut. The former Broadway cars were arranged in rows, some of their windows boarded up and their doors (needlessly) made to swing instead of slide. Thus a summer camp arose practically overnight on Long Island Sound, given the highfalutin name of Avon Park Heights.† In some instances a pair of

* *American Notes for General Circulation*, London, 1842, p. 170.
† *House Beautiful*, November 1905, p. 64.

73. *Jacob Heyman's house, Carville, California.*

cars was attached at right angles for a two-room house. The wheels of course were taken off and the vehicles raised on stilts three or four feet off the ground, necessitated by the sandy soil. The elevation also provided a better view and more privacy. Nobody bothered much to call the colony by its rightful name when the more descriptive "Carville" would do just as well.

Other carvilles mushroomed elsewhere along the Atlantic seaboard and on the lakes and rivers, wherever a city's public service improvement program made horse trams obsolete and eager inhabitants desired cozy vacation shelters ready-made.

The most famous camp in America sprang up almost in the shadow of San Francisco's Cliff House. It was variously called Ocean Side, Ozonia, or (again) Carville. Carville, California, was the private enterprise of Jacob Heyman, who first purchased a number of cast-off cars from the street-railway companies of San Francisco for ten dollars apiece. In January, 1899, one of these was sold to a Mr. George Robinson, together with a strip of land, for $650.* The price included delivery of the car. This was only the beginning. Others went readily, and the laying out of a small beach town was under way. Here, too, the cars were put up on posts after the wheels had been discarded. Some buyers paid a little more to obtain two or three cars. The practice here was to remove adjoining sides and leash the cars together laterally. At best the streetcar camps provided constricted quarters.

The notable edifice in this village of Lilliputian houses was Jacob Heyman's own residence, called "Dad's Home." It was composed of six cars incorporated into a two-storied structure that stood on a platform. The cars were interspersed between constructed forms, and combined into a low wing to one side. The effect was a cross

* *Country Life in America,* March 1907, p. 492.

between a seaside Shangri-la and a railroad pile-up. One wonders whether Mom Hey-man called the family from the beach for the evening meal by shouting: "First call for dinner!"; or maybe to get them in she pulled the cord and clanged the trolley bell, supplementing the act by a lusty vocalization of "All aboard!"

JAPANESE AEROPLANE BUNGALOW

CONEY ISLAND has seen better days—or, perhaps, one should say, better nights. Once, crowds jammed the boats and trams bound to and from this land of enchantment during the summer months. Visitors to New York did not consider their stay complete without a trip to Coney Island. Now it is quite otherwise: the amusement attractions have deteriorated, so that only the glassed-in Steeplechase bravely carries on the Coney tradition; and the beach and broadwalk—except on holidays—have reverted to the local inhabitants, who continue to patronize the hot corn, hot dog, hot knishes, ice cream, cold pop, and frozen custard concessions, and instinctively carry with them to the surf their blankets, beach chairs, umbrellas, radios, portable televi-sions, newspapers and books, bottles of oil, lotion and sun-tan spray, and large bags filled with edibles brought from home.

Let us go back to a time before this—but not so far back as when Walt Whitman walked quietly along Coney's "long bare unfrequented shore"—rather to that interven-ing period during which was centered here the cult of uninhibited hilarity, when thousands paid admission-coin tribute to the speculators of fun and merriment, to be caught up in a whirl of excitement and jostled and precipitated into a new, uncensored perspective. The mobs sought entertainment, illusion, and escape, and the place that fulfilled these needs best was one of the three big amusement parks, such as "Dreamland," the rival to Luna Park and Steeplechase, opened to the public in 1904. It stood on the site of the present Aquarium. A strange "park" it was, without a tree or a blade of grass, as devoid of greenery as Times Square or Wall Street. Visitors obviously did not come here to commune with nature; they came, instead, to explore this never-never land, riotous with blinking lights and brilliant colors, bizarre architectural effects, and intriguing labyrinths of love and distraction, where they might dispel their feelings of loneliness or boredom with the workaday world. This was most assuredly the right spot for the exhibition of that recently tested machine heralding new vistas of adven-ture and travel, the airplane—or "aeroplane," as it used to be called. A man (really

74. Air Ship Building, "Dreamland," Coney Island.
After a photograph in *Bungalow Magazine*, August 1916.

two men) had succeeded in raising himself off the ground in a self-powered, heavier-than-air contraption for the first time in December of 1903, and although few sensible newspapers recorded the event, the achievement of Wilbur and Orville Wright at Kitty Hawk was just the thing to touch off the imagination of revelers seeking diversion in an amusement park. Here was a new wonder for them to examine. Equally remarkable as the exhibit inside was the building housing it. Located near the bridge at the base of the long chute down which the flat-bottomed boats came zipping to splash across the lagoon occupying the center of the midway quadrangle, the structure displaying the air ship was Japanese in style. No other building in the park was Japanese; but, then, all of them being different it fitted in very nicely with the theme of diversity and variety.

75. *The Aeroplane Bungalow of the De Luxe Build-*
ing Company, Los Angeles.
After a photograph in *Bungalow Magazine,* August
1916.

Japanese architecture already had put in an appearance along the Atlantic seaboard, in the Nippon House at the Philadelphia Centennial of 1876, in the residence built for a Unitarian minister (who had previously visited Japan) at Fall River, Massachusetts, during the mid 1890's, and in a large dwelling constructed by a New York realtor (who anticipated its proving to be "a good seller") near Prospect Park, Brooklyn, in 1902.* Except for the fact that the first was at a fair, there was nothing about these examples that could have prompted the mode selected for the Dreamland hall—especially in having to do with its housing an airplane. In looking around for a building that might have some bearing upon the matter our attention is arrested by the Japanese entry at the World's Columbian Exposition at Chicago in 1892–93. Called the Hō-ō-dō, or "Phoenix Hall," the Chicago building was modeled after the famous mid-eleventh-cen-

* The author's "The American Bungalow," *Art Bulletin,* September 1958, p. 252.

tury Phoenix Temple at Uji. The original suggests a giant bird, with wings outstretched and having a long tail, placed upon a tiny island so that the still waters of the lake reflect clouds, giving it the appearance of being suspended in the sky. The influence of the Hō-ō-dō upon subsequent American architecture was tremendous, as upon the work of Frank Lloyd Wright, who, around 1900, adopted the cruciform house plan that came to be called the "airplane plan."* The house Wright built in 1908 for E. H. Gilmore at Madison, Wisconsin, is still universally referred to as the "Airplane House." The bird-form building of Old Japan thus became linked with the new American flying machine, which, in a round-about way of reasoning, may explain why at Coney Island a Japanese-type building should have been chosen to shelter the airplane.

* The author's "Japanese Buildings in the United States before 1900: Their Influence upon American Domestic Architecture," *Art Bulletin*, September 1953, pp. 221–22.

The Coney Island essay in Far Eastern architecture exerted some force too, notably in the house built by and for "The Queen of the Air," Blanche Sloan, at Jamaica, Long Island, in 1909. The builder was no aviatrix, as her title might suggest, but an aerialist famous in her day for breathtaking feats on the flying trapeze. Her three-storied frame house resembled the top of the pagoda-like tower of the airship building. It was featured on the front cover of the *Bungalow Magazine* for January 1910, in which issue it was described as a Japanese "Torri"—sounding like something out of Carmen, but evidently a mistake in spelling for *torii,* which, however, is Japanese for a cere-monial gateway and is never applied to a dwelling. Blanche Sloan toured Europe making frequent professional appearances in order to raise the money to erect the Long Island retreat, but then spent most of it on laces and other conceits catching her fancy, and had to pick up hammer and saw herself to help build her dream house.

The Japanese style made its biggest conquest on the West Coast, where it soon became synonymous for "California House," nowadays *alias dictus* (incorrectly) as "ranch style." Shortly after the beginning of the present century the architecture of the island empire became the chief determining factor in the design of the small house we designate the bungalow, specimens of which sprang up all over southern California, and of course spread elsewhere throughout the country. The finest by common consent were those built by the two brothers, Charles Sumner and Henry Mather Greene, but many builders drew from the same source of inspiration. Most of them had not the faintest concept of the principles involved in Eastern building and merely made use of externals for an unusual effect, which turned out to be, more often than not, visually unacceptable.

Just before World War I the De Luxe Building Company of Los Angeles erected a house called the "Aeroplane Bungalow." It was in Japanese style, being low, with much exposed timberwork, and upturned ends to the very deep eaves of the roofs. Chimneys and porch pier bases were of cobblestones. The living room across the front was supple-mented by two recesses in the corners set on axis with the diagonals of the room. One of these contained the big fireplace, and a porch lay between them. Behind the living room were dining and breakfast rooms, and beyond the latter a kitchen and maid's room. Two bedrooms and a bath were at the back of the house. A stairway in the passage led up to the featured element: *"flying bedrooms"*—chambers on the second floor over-looking the rooftops of the fore part of the house, with multiple, fluttering eaves giving some excuse for the designation pertaining to the air-borne dormitories. Taken literally, one would have reason to expect nocturnal excursions among the stars, but the house did not go soaring off into space either as a whole or in sections. Its affinity to the airplane was as romantic as the shaping of its lines after those of an Oriental building—not as relevant, actually, the latter at least constituting architectonic forms. The "Japanese Aeroplane Bungalow" was a heterogeneous concoction prompted by rank commercialism bidding for sales through appealing to two different fads that chanced to be raging at the same time.

EPILOGUE: FOLLIES AD INFINITUM

IN THE preceding pages there has been reviewed a number of examples of the curiosa of American building. It is not to be imagined that this discussion exhausts the subject. Far from it: there are indeed many more specimens that could be included with equal justification.* It just so happens that the ones selected here—for one reason or another—are special pets of the author. It will have been found that the majority predate the present century, which is due to the fact that architectural follies, like Chinese eggs, take on more savour with the passage of time. Except for naming a few round houses of the early 1900's (Chapter VII, Part 1) and discussing the later Corn Palace (Chapter XI, Part 1), all references to recent buildings are confined to the last two chapters, and primarily to the chapter immediately before this one, stressing new developments in the folly field.

I would like to digress for just one moment to say that there are other constructions fabricated of unusual materials related to the bottle houses lately dealt with. One of these is an oyster-shell house at Spotswood, New Jersey, built by Gustave Osterberg, (as one might expect) a sea-food dealer. A two-storied, eight-room house at Petersburg, Virginia, was built by O. E. Young out of old tombstones. (The situation would have been ideal had the structure only been put up in a ghost town.) W. G. Brown conceived an office of petrified wood at Lamar, Colorado; and there is a house hollowed out of a redwood stump at Eureka, California.

In line with the streetcar summer-cottage idea, two brothers converted an old interurban car into quarters while attending the University of West Virginia during the 1940's. A ranch house near Medora, North Dakota, had been a Pullman coach, surfaced

---

* Such as "Körner's Folly," the J. Gilmer Körner house-studio-and-little-theatre built about 1880 in Kernersville, North Carolina (Blackwell P. Robinson, *The North Carolina Guide*, Chapel Hill, 1955, p. 515), and the mysteriously abandoned Ostrander house at Paint Rock, Texas (*Coronet*, December 1956, pp. 85–88), also dating from the end of the nineteenth century.

with cobblestones. Similar adaptations include the home of Jessie E. Pearson, formerly a bridge across the Blackwater River, in Virginia, and the round faculty house at the University of Wyoming, which had been a water tank for an orphanage.*

Another type of unusual structure, not previously noted, is descended from the old Southern "shoo-fly," a platform built in a tree, with a staircase leading up to it, a sort

* Examples included in the last two paragraphs were published in various issues of *Bruce Magazine*, 1947–50.

76. The Paul Doullut houses, New Orleans, Louisiana.

of away-from-the-house piazza. Such an arrangement, designed by Max Schroff, was perched in the branches of a tree over a rustic mountain lodge on Rock River, Wisconsin, during the early 1880's; and a fifteen-foot square *enclosed* house, set on a wide deck in a buttonwood, forty feet above the ground, was constructed by Morton B. Ewing at Hellan, Pennsylvania, in 1920.*

But my real business here, in winding up this exposé on American architectural od-

* *American Architect and Building News,* 9 June 1883, n. p.; *Bruce Magazine,* Winter 1948, p. 16.

dities, is to reveal the fact that the precedent set in the eighteenth and nineteenth centuries still persists in the twentieth. No better demonstration of this fact can be cited than in the culminating example of the steamboat-house rage, discussed in Chapter VI. When Paul Doullut, a former steamboat captain, started to build himself a home overlooking the Mississippi River, in the east suburbs of New Orleans, in 1905, it is only natural that he would plan it with decks all around and put a pilothouse-belvedere on top. He even resorted to metal smokestack chimneys, which none of the nineteenth-

77. Dick's Castle, near Garrison-on-Hudson, New York.

century steamboat houses had manifested. There was another strong influence that cropped up in this residence, however, and it was prompted by an exhibit at the Saint Louis Louisiana Purchase Exposition of 1903–4. There, in the Japanese Imperial Garden, was built a replica of the late-fourteenth-century Kinkaku, or "Golden Pavilion," the original a villa near Kyoto, conceived for the Shogun Yoshimitsu, a three-storied building with delicate encircling porches, the topmost story considerably smaller than the first and second. The flaring roofs of the Japanese villa were conspicuously repeated in the design of the Doullut house. More original features are: the white-glazed terracotta walls and columns of the ground floor and the decorative use made of wooden balls, graded in size (like the pearls of a necklace) and strung on steel wires between the posts of the upper gallery. Quite steamboat-like are the careful joinery of the framed second and third stories, the prominent display of outside staircases, and the narrow passages and steep stairways inside. An exact duplicate of the house was built later for a son nearby. Because of their styling and period the two houses may be referred to as Japanese-steamboat bungalows. The only voyage these steamers ever made was when they were moved back from the river several hundred feet at the time the levee was extended along this stretch of the Mississippi.

While on the subject of steamboats, it might be well to mention that the forty-four-room mansion at 2020 Massachusetts Avenue, N. W., in Washington, D. C., designed by Henry Anderson and built for Thomas F. Walsh, in 1902–3, contained a Y-shaped staircase in the great hall, that was inspired by a similar arrangement in the steamer on which the Walshes traveled to Europe. During this period there had come into being a short-lived phase of lush interior decoration that went by the name of "North German Lloyd," and the Walsh mansion sported its full share of the new styling.* In 1940 the building became the district quarters of the Red Cross and a decade later was taken over by the Indonesian Embassy.

"Lord" Timothy Dexter's outdoor figure gallery of historical personages is recalled by a depository of American history begun in Arkansas in 1920. The financier William Hope ("Coin") Harvey, erstwhile counselor to William Jennings Bryan, retired to a remote spot in the Ozarks, where he set out to build a pyramid or obelisk, that would contain the records of what he fancied, at the time, to be a civilization headed for sure ruin. His cue for preserving records evidently was taken from the Egyptians. He raised about $10,000 as a starter on his $75,000 project; but the obelisk never rose any higher than the foundations, because the Depression hit at the end of the twenties, and when the Depression was over it looked as though the country was going to survive after all. Harvey's was a sort of one-man Tower of Babel. At the time of the financier's death in 1936 there was left behind a lot of stonework, near Monte Ne, that resembled an amphitheatre; and that is exactly what it was taken over and used for, by the members of Camp Joyzelle, a vacation development for young girls.

Another unfinished folly is the castle located on a hilltop overlooking the Hudson River several miles north of Garrison, New York. This is a section of the country addicted to follies, Fishkill (site of Fowler's Folly) lying ten miles due north, Irvington (the

---

* See Evelyn McLean, *Father Struck It Rich*, Boston, 1936, p. 92.

Bonnet House) and Tarrytown (Paulding's Folly) being twenty-five miles to the south, and only a few miles upstream from Garrison, on an island in the river, stands Bannerman's Arsenal, a late-nineteenth-century cardboard castle built of brick and stone, serving as a warehouse for Francis Bannerman's New York emporium of old armor, swords, guns, and other armaments. Work on the nearby castle for Evans R. Dick was begun in 1905, and came to a standstill in 1917. The architectural style of the house, slated to cost $1,250,000 and estimated to have come to $500,000 when work was abandoned, was inspired by Moorish buildings seen by the Dicks along the Mediterranean. Employing mainly steel and concrete, the materials of the Hudson River villa could not have been more foreign either to the source of design inspiration or to the resources of the locality itself, every ounce of metal and every grain of lime going into the structure having to be carted up the mountainside. The irregular pile stretches out 180 feet in one direction and 220 feet in another, one tower rising 86 feet above ground level. The property was bought for a factory in 1944, and recently the new owner made liveable, and moved into, one of the forty-two rooms the castle was intended to contain. The word, "intended," is used here because the only existing internal divisions in the house are the floors, the system of construction making it possible for this to be so. Being devoid of partition walls the structure seems more like a factory than a place of habitation, and perhaps is coming into its rightful destiny. An alternative proposal is its becoming a museum of minerals. The enterprising teen-age daughter of the present tenant admits visitors to look around "Dick's Folly" for a quarter a head on Sundays and holidays, laying aside the proceeds towards a college education.*

Perhaps mention, at least, should be made of the F. W. Bennett *folie* at Hamburg, New Jersey, which, to the tune of $250,000, took the form of a gingerbread castle.† And at Storytown, four miles south of Lake George in upper New York state, is to be found a facsimile of the home of the old woman who lived in the shoe, and other nursery favorites.‡ On a much greater scale is that most lucrative of folly layouts inspired by the realm of fairy legends, Disneyland, in southern California. More engaging as a folly, because of its former exclusiveness, is the not-too-far-away San Simeon, the William Randolph Hearst home and ranch, that spreads out over 430 square miles, with its private flying field, game preserve, tennis courts, and swimming pools, four guest houses modeled after French châteaux, and, on the summit of La Cuesta Encantada ("The Enchanted Hill"), La Casa Grande, or main house itself, Spanish in style, sur-

* *New York Sun*, 22 June 1940, p. 36; *New York Times*, 7 April 1955, p. L 29.
† *Bruce Magazine*, March-April 1951, p. /12/.
‡ *Better Homes & Gardens*, July 1958, p. 49.

rounded by Italian gardens, complete with an abundance of marble statuary, marble balustraded terraces and staircases, garden temples, and tiled pools.* The long refectory table in the dining hall of the Casa often accommodated eighty persons at dinner, after which all guests were required to attend the cinema shown in the host's private theatre. There were other do's and don't's imposed upon the guests by their eccentric host, such as having no liquor in the bedrooms and refraining from mentioning the word "death."

* *Harper's Bazaar*, July 1955, pp. /38–43/.

78. Sam Hill's Folly, Columbia River, Washington.

San Simeon was opened as a public park and museum by the California Historical Society in the spring of 1958.*

A West Coast complement to Dick's Castle is a mock Flemish Renaissance castle, that stands above "America's Rhine," the Columbia River, in Washington. The big house was begun in 1913 by Sam Hill, an enterprising pioneer in railroad and highway building, operating in Russia and Japan, as well as in this country. He often boasted that he

* Oscar Lewis, *Fabulous San Simeon*, San Francisco, 1958.

was partly responsible for the fortunes of Henry Ford and John D. Rockefeller. As a youth, Sam Hill had attended the University of Munich, and there his roommate, incognito at first, turned out to be none other than Albert, crown prince of Belgium, who later often entertained his American friend at the palace in Brussels. Another of Sam Hill's royal friends was Queen Marie of Roumania. Hill built his first castle at Seattle in 1909, as a place in which to receive Prince Albert properly, when he came to visit the Alaska-Yukon Pacific Exposition; but the death of King Leopold prevented the crown prince from ever reaching Seattle or Hill's first castle. The second castle was begun above the great gash of the Columbia River four years later. A classic Flemish pile, with balustrades encompassing the flat roofs, it was constructed to last a millennium, the structural method resembling that of Dick's Castle. The only wood used inside was for floors, and these were laid atop a six-inch steel and concrete sub-flooring. There were twenty-eight suites of rooms, including a dining hall that could seat 250 persons. The house was equipped with two electric elevators and eight dumb waiters. In 1922 Sam Hill decided to convert the building into a museum of fine arts, and, although unfinished, Queen Marie dedicated it as such during her tour of the United States in 1926. Here the queen deposited her coronation crown and gown, her throne and audience chair, her gold and silver filigree dresser set, and many other personal treasures, saying that they would be safer in America than in Europe.* Completion of the mansion awaited the approach of the highway; but when Sam Hill died in 1931 the engineers had laid a road only to within a half-mile of the gates. The interiors were installed under the direction of the trustees. "Maryhill" was the name given to the house by the builder, but, more often than not, it subsequently has been referred to as "Sam Hill's Folly."

A folly named after a folly is Fonthill, the original being the late-eighteenth-century make-believe castle of William Beckford, Fonthill Abbey (see note p. 76), in England. The Fonthill in the United States is on East Court Street at the edge of Doylestown, Pennsylvania. It was built during the first quarter of the twentieth century for Dr. Henry C. Mercer, one-time Curator of American and Prehistoric Archeology at the University of Pennsylvania, and a manufacturer of pottery and tile. The towering, château-like residence of concrete and stone presents a wavering outline due to having been constructed without aid of either straightedge or plumb bob. The builder believed the human eye to be sufficiently capable of erecting satisfactory uprights and horizontals without resorting to mechanical aids. Dr. Mercer scheduled his day according to sunlight, and the walls of his home were pierced by oversized windows. No elec-

* The *Providence Sunday Journal*, 19 May 1940, p. 2.

tricity was allowed in the house. Nearby stands the pottery works, a U-shaped building styled after ancient structures in Yucatan. Both house and factory make use of glazed tiles on the roofs. Dr. Mercer was the benefactor of the Bucks County Historical Society, which occupies two buildings at Pine and Ashland streets in Doylestown.

Just as America has nurtured its Brownes, Dexters, Harrises, and Morrises of the eighteenth century, its Croghans, Pittses, Barnums, Nutts, Southwicks, Fowlers, Mays, and Wrights of the early to mid nineteenth century, its Draughans, Galbraiths, Chadwicks, Palmers, Floods, and Laffertys of the late nineteenth century, and its Ilgs, Doulluts, Dicks, Harveys, Hills, and Mercers of the first half of the twentieth, so, undoubtedly, this country will bring forth other prospective folly-builders to perpetuate this spirited tradition. As was disclosed in the Prologue, the author has dabbled in concocting a few himself and is impeded only by lack of means to carrying them into realization. The cult, therefore, will have to be continued by other persons in whom imagination and the wherewithal are happily coexisting. So, if you happen to have both of these prerequisites, then it is up to you to carry on this great American pastime, by adding to its accumulated store. If you do not happen to find just the right novel idea for your own architectural folly among the existing examples herein described, then you are invited to contact the author for an appropriate and dazzling suggestion.

THE END

APPENDIX 3

A GEOGRAPHIC GUIDE TO AMERICAN FOLLIES

(arranged alphabetically by state and place)

ALABAMA: *Mobile,* steamboat drawing room in former Le Vert house; pp. 111–12.

Uniontown, Pitts' Folly, built for Phillip Henry Pitts in 1852–53; pp. 72, 73, 75.

ARIZONA: *Tombstone,* Cochise County Courthouse, built in 1882; pp. 160–62.

ARKANSAS: *Monte Ne,* "Coin" Harvey's monument to history, 1920–29, unfinished; p. 228.

CALIFORNIA: *Anaheim,* Disneyland, on Santa Ana Freeway; p. 229.

Eureka, redwood-stump house; p. 223.

Los Angeles, Brant mansion, 3131 South Figueroa Street, built in 1884 (recently used as dormitory by University of Southern California).

Los Angeles, Japanese Aeroplane Bungalow, conceived by the De Luxe Building Company about 1915; p. 220.

Menlo Park, Linden Towers, James Clair Flood's wooden mansion completed in 1879 (destroyed); pp. 168, 169, 171, 172.

Palo Alto, windmill residence of Mrs. R. N. Wilcox.

San Francisco, Wright's Folly, Renaissance Revival bank building designed by Peter Portois and built for Stephen Wright during 1850's (destroyed during earthquake of 1906); pp. 154–57.

San Francisco, Vedanta Center, an ornate Oriental architectural extravaganza built in 1905; pp. 205–6.

San Francisco, Carville, Jacob Heyman's streetcar settlement beneath Cliff House, begun 1899; pp. 215–16.

San Jose, Winchester mystery house, Sarah Winchester's country house that continued to be added to from the mid 1880's until 1922 (now a museum, Los Gatos Road); pp. 172–77.

San Simeon, La Casa Grande, William Randolph Hearst's palace begun in 1919 (now a museum); pp. 229–31.

Watts (Los Angeles), Simon Rida's scrap-metal towers (up to 150 feet tall).

COLORADO: *Lamar,* W. G. Brown's petrified-wood office; p. 223.

CONNECTICUT: *Avon Park Heights (Bridgeport),* Carville, streetcar summer camp, around 1900; pp. 214–15.

Bridgeport, Iranistan, Phineas Taylor Barnum's Oriental villa designed by Leopold Eidlitz of New York City and built in 1848 (destroyed by fire in 1857); pp. 18, 87–90, 91, 93–97.

Greenwich, I. N. Phelps Stokes' sixteenth-century house imported from Suffolk County, England, in 1911, added to his home on Stockridge Mountain (sold and moved into town); p. 203.

Tonopah, William F. Peck's beer-bottle house, 1902; p. 212.

NEW JERSEY: *Hamburg,* F. W. Bennett's gingerbread castle (for children); p. 229.

Margate City, Elephant Hotel built by the inventor, James V. Lafferty, about 1883; pp. 191, 194.

Spotswood, oyster-shell house of Gustave Osterberg; p. 223.

NEW YORK: *Barrytown,* mock gothic ruin built for John Church Cruger during mid nineteenth century on Cruger's Island; p. 79.

Clayton, Boldt's Castle, Alexandria Bay, for George F. Boldt, never finished.

Coney Island, Dreamland, an amusement park built in 1904 (burned in 1911); pp. 216–19.

Coney Island, Elephantine Colossus or Elephant Hotel, built by James V. Lafferty during 1880's (burned in 1896); p. 196.

Fishkill, Fowler's Folly, octagonal villa of Orson Squire Fowler, phrenologist, writer, lecturer, and publisher, designed by owner, 1848 (demolished in 1897); pp. 134, 135, 137–39.

Garrison-on-Hudson, Dick's Castle, Evans R. Dick's Moorish villa, 1905–17 (unfinished); pp. 227–29, 231.

Irvington-on-Hudson, Philip Armour's octagonal house of about 1860, enlarged and embellished by Joseph Stiver; p. 141.

Jamaica, Oaka Hall, Blanche Sloan's Japanese "Torri" or summer house, 1909; p. 220.

Lake George, Storytown; p. 229.

New York City, Smith's Folly, 421 East 61 Street, unfinished residence begun 1799 (stone stable alone standing).

Ossining, Arthur S. Vernal's house, parts imported from England, 1913; p. 203.

Poughkeepsie, John E. Brinckerhoff (builder of the "Mary Powell") house, steamboat style, 1880's.

Tarrytown, Paulding's Folly, castellated house built for Philip Paulding in 1841; pp. 79, 229.

NORTH CAROLINA: *Kernersville,* Körner's Folly, studio-theatre house of J. Gilmer Körner built about 1880; p. 223 fn.

NORTH DAKOTA: *Medora,* Pullman-coach house covered with cobblestones; pp. 223–24.

OHIO: *Cincinnati,* Trollope's Folly, bazaar built in Oriental style for Frances Trollope in 1829 (demolished end of nineteenth century); pp. 18, 82–87.

Cincinnati (Walnut Hills section), Fisher châlet, a Swiss-style house designed by Lucien F. Plympton for A. D. Fisher; pp. 198, 199.

Columbus, Kelley's Folly, built about 1839; pp. 72, 75.

PENNSYLVANIA: *Doylestown,* Fonthill, Dr. Henry C. Mercer's concrete, stone, and tile château built during the early 1900's; pp. 232–33.

Hellan, Morton B. Ewing's tree house, 1920; p. 225.

New Hope, Cintra or Maris' Folly, built for William Maris about 1816 (now antique shop); pp. 65, 66, 137.

Philadelphia, The Marble Palace or Morris' Folly, built by Pierre Charles l'Enfant for Robert Morris during 1790's at Chestnut and Seventh streets (razed before completion shortly after 1800); pp. 62, 63, 65, 66.

Pittsburgh, Picnic House or Croghan's Folly, built on Black Horse Hill for parties of William Croghan's daughter during 1830's and enlarged for her residence during 1840's (obliterated except for one room, moved to Cathedral of Learning, University of Pittsburgh); pp. 66, 69, 70.

RHODE ISLAND: *Jamestown,* late-nineteenth-century shingled round house of Daniel S. Newhall designed by Charles Follen McKim; p. 128.

Middletown, Southwick house, the frame, drum-shaped residence built by Joseph or Christopher Southwick (shipwrights) about 1841; pp. 125, 126, 127.

SOUTH CAROLINA: *Milford* (near Stateburg), Manning's Folly, built about 1850; p. 75.

SOUTH DAKOTA: *Mitchell,* corn palaces, public halls decorated with grain murals, first one built in 1892, second one begun in 1921, styled after a maharaja's palace; pp. 180–85.

TEXAS: *Mineral Wells,* Hexagon House, twelve-sided hotel built by David G. Galbraith in 1897; pp. 2, 145–50.

Paint Rock, Ostrander house, the mysteriously abandoned end-of-the-nineteenth-century residence of W. B. Ostrander; p. 223 fn.

Texarkana, Draughan's Folly, an ace-of-clubs design built by J. H. Draughan in 1884; pp. 142, 144, 145.

VIRGINIA: *Hillsville,* John W. Hope's bottle house; p. 213.

Lynchburg, Poplar Forest, Thomas Jefferson's octagonal retreat (burned during mid nineteenth century and partially rebuilt); pp. 131, 132, 133.

Petersburg, O. E. Young's house of tombstones; p. 223.

Petersburg, Trapezium Place, irregular polygonal house built for Charles O'hara in 1815; p. 133.

Richmond, Winsor Farms, fourteenth-century Lancashire manor re-erected for T. C. Williams, Jr., in 1925; p. 203.

Staunton, The Folly, Lee Highway, built by Joseph Smith in 1818.

Eastern Shore, Bowman's Folly.

WASHINGTON: *Columbia River,* Maryhill or Sam Hill's Folly, a Flemish Renaissance castle begun in 1913 (now a museum); pp. 231, 232.

WISCONSIN: *Lake Geneva,* Ceylon Court, a villa rebuilt from the Singhalese pavilion at the World's Columbian Exposition in Chicago, 1892–93; pp. 201–3.

Milton, hexagonal house of Joseph Goodrich, 1845; pp. 138–39, 141, 147.

Rock River, Max Schroff's tree house, 1880's; p. 225.

WYOMING: *Laramie,* round faculty house at the University of Wyoming, formerly a water tank for an orphanage; p. 224.

INDEX

Entries in small caps are names of
architectural follies.